daybook, *n.* a book in which the events of the day are recorded; *specif.* a journal or diary

DAYBOOK
of Critical Reading and Writing

CONSULTING AUTHORS

FRAN CLAGGETT

LOUANN REID

RUTH VINZ

Great Source Education Group
a Houghton Mifflin Company
Wilmington, Massachusetts

www.greatsource.com

The Consulting Authors

Fran Claggett, currently an educational consultant for schools throughout the country and teacher at Sonoma State University, taught high school English for more than thirty years. She is author of several books, including *Drawing Your Own Conclusions: Graphic Strategies for Reading, Writing, and Thinking* (1992) and *A Measure of Success* (1996).

Louann Reid taught junior and senior high school English, speech, and drama for nineteen years and currently teaches courses for future English teachers at Colorado State University. Author of numerous articles and chapters, her first books were *Learning the Landscape* and *Recasting the Text* with Fran Claggett and Ruth Vinz (1996).

Ruth Vinz, currently a professor and director of English education at Teachers College, Columbia University, taught in secondary schools for twenty-three years. She is author of several books and numerous articles that discuss teaching and learning in the English classroom as well as a frequent presenter, consultant, and co-teacher in schools throughout the country.

Printed in the United States of America

International Standard Book Number: 0-669-46440-6

7 8 9 10 - RRDW - 04 03 02

3

4

Focus/Strategy	Lesson	Author/Literature

7

Angles of Literacy

Literacy means being able to understand what you read. It also means being able to talk about your ideas with other people. "Angles" are different ways to help you become more literate. Throughout this *Daybook*, you'll be asked to read and respond to many different kinds of literature. You'll circle, underline, and highlight. You'll make guesses, ask questions, and think about word meanings. You'll draw pictures, brainstorm, and do some writing of your own. In short, you'll look at what you read and what you write in many different ways. You'll learn to respond to literature in a whole new way by becoming an active reader.

One Becoming an Active Reader

Active readers get involved in what they read. One of the simplest ways to become involved—to make the selection "your own"—is to mark up the page with questions, reactions, and ideas. Circle words that seem interesting or strange. Underline sentences that might be meaningful and write "Wow!" in the margin. Highlight important information. Draw boxes around phrases that are confusing and mark the sections with a "Huh?" As you read this piece by Mildred D. Taylor, notice how one active reader became involved in the selection.

Response Notes

Like Mildred Taylor?

huh?

Taylor's background

slavery

wow!

sounds like my father

"Author's Note" from *Roll of Thunder, Hear My Cry*
by Mildred D. Taylor

My father was a master storyteller. He could tell a fine old story that made me hold my sides with rolling laughter and sent happy tears down my cheeks, or a story of stark reality that made me shiver and be grateful for my own warm, secure surroundings. He could tell stories of beauty and grace, stories of gentle dreams, and paint them as vividly as any picture with splashes of character and dialogue. His memory detailed every event of ten or forty years or more before, just as if it had happened yesterday.

By the fireside in our northern home or in the South where I was born, I learned a history not then written in books but one passed from generation to generation on the steps of moonlit porches and beside dying fires in one-room houses, a history of great-grandparents and of slavery and of the days following slavery; of those who lived still not free, yet who would not let their spirits be enslaved. From my father the storyteller I learned to respect the past, to respect my own heritage and myself. From my father the man I learned even more, for he was endowed with a special grace that made him tower above other men. He was warm and steadfast, a man whose principles would not bend, and he had within him a rare strength that sustained not only my sister and me and all the family but all those who sought his advice and leaned upon his wisdom.

He was a complex person, yet he taught me many simple things, things important for a child to know: how to ride a horse and how to skate; how to blow soap bubbles and how to tie a kite knot that met the challenge of the March winds; how to bathe a huge faithful mongrel dog named Tiny. In time, he taught me the complex things too. He taught me of myself, of life. He taught me of hopes and dreams. And he taught me the love of words. Without his teachings, without his words, my words would not have been.

10

"Author's Note" from *Roll of Thunder, Hear My Cry*
by Mildred D. Taylor

My father died last week. The stories as only he could tell them died with him. But his voice of joy and laughter, his enduring strength, his principles and constant wisdom remain, a part of all those who knew and loved him well. They remain also within the pages of this book, its guiding spirit and total power.

> As you read this excerpt from *Roll of Thunder, Hear My Cry,* underline, circle, make notes, insert exclamations, ask questions, answer questions, draw doodles—whatever strikes you as you read.

from *Roll of Thunder, Hear My Cry* by Mildred D. Taylor

"Little Man, would you come on? You keep it up and you're gonna make us late."

My youngest brother paid no attention to me. Grasping more firmly his newspaper-wrapped notebook and his tin-can lunch of cornbread and oil sausages, he continued to concentrate on the dusty road. He lagged several feet behind my other brothers, Stacey and Christopher-John, and me, attempting to keep the rusty Mississippi dust from swelling with each step and drifting back upon his shiny black shoes and the cuffs of his corduroy pants by lifting each foot high before setting it gently down again. Always meticulously neat, six-year-old Little Man never allowed dirt or tears or stains to mar anything he owned. Today was no exception.

"You keep it up and make us late for school, Mama's gonna wear you out," I threatened, pulling with exasperation at the high collar of the Sunday dress Mama had made me wear for the first day of school—as if that event were something special. It seemed to me that showing up at school at all on a bright August-like October morning made for running the cool forest trails and wading barefoot in the forest pond was concession enough; Sunday clothing was asking too much. Christopher-John and Stacey were not too pleased about the clothing or school either. Only Little Man, just beginning his school career, found the prospects of both intriguing.

"Y'all go ahead and get dirty if y'all wanna," he replied without even looking up from his studied steps. "Me, I'm gonna stay clean."

"I betcha Mama's gonna 'clean' you, you keep it up," I grumbled.

"Ah Cassie, leave him be," Stacey admonished, frowning and kicking testily at the road.

from *Roll of Thunder, Hear My Cry* by Mildred D. Taylor

"I ain't said nothing but—"

Stacey cut me a wicked look and I grew silent. His disposition had been irritatingly sour lately. If I hadn't known the cause of it, I could have forgotten very easily that he was, at twelve, bigger than I, and that I had promised Mama to arrive at school looking clean and ladylike. "Shoot," I mumbled finally, unable to restrain myself from further comment, "it ain't my fault you gotta be in Mama's class this year."

Stacey's frown deepened and he jammed his fists into his pockets, but said nothing.

Christopher-John, walking between Stacey and me, glanced uneasily at both of us but did not interfere. A short, round boy of seven, he took little interest in troublesome things, preferring to remain on good terms with everyone. Yet he was always sensitive to others and now, shifting the handle of his lunch can from his right hand to his right wrist and his smudged notebook from his left hand to his left armpit, he stuffed his free hands into his pockets and attempted to make his face as moody as Stacey's and as cranky as mine. But after a few moments he seemed to forget that he was supposed to be grouchy and began whistling cheerfully. There was little that could make Christopher-John unhappy for very long, not even the thought of school.

I tugged again at my collar and dragged my feet in the dust, allowing it to sift back onto my socks and shoes like gritty red snow. I hated the dress. And the shoes. There was little I could do in a dress, and as for shoes, they imprisoned freedom-loving feet accustomed to the feel of the warm earth.

"Cassie, stop that," Stacey snapped as the dust billowed in swirling clouds around my feet. I looked up sharply, ready to protest. Christopher-John's whistling increased to a raucous, nervous shrill, and grudgingly I let the matter drop and trudged along in moody silence, my brothers growing as pensively quiet as I.

Before us the narrow, sun-splotched road wound like a lazy red serpent dividing the high forest bank of quiet, old trees on the left from the cotton field, forested by giant green-and-purple stalks, on the right. A barbed-wire fence ran the length of the deep field, stretching eastward for over a quarter of a mile until it met the sloping green pasture that signaled the end of our family's four hundred acres. An ancient oak tree on the slope, visible even now, was the official dividing mark between Logan land and the beginning of a dense forest. Beyond the protective fencing of the forest, vast farming fields, worked by a multitude of share-cropping families, covered two thirds of a ten-square-mile plantation. That was Harlan Granger land.

12

In a small group, discuss the excerpt. Before you begin, review the questions and comments you noted in the margin of your book.

●◆ Use the discussion to do a quickwrite about your reaction to Mildred Taylor's story. What do you think of it so far? What do you find most interesting? What do you react to most strongly?

Quickwrite: My Thoughts About the Story

13

Make a selection "your own" by jotting notes in the margin, highlighting words and phrases that seem important, and underlining words or ideas you don't understand.

Two
Connecting with the Story

How does a reader "connect" with a story? One way is to compare the story to your own life. If you read about a baby-sitting fiasco, think about your most recent baby-sitting job. If you read a story about a boy who strikes out time and again, think about a recent baseball game you played in or watched. Being reminded of the experiences you've had—or the experiences you'd like to have—helps you to be involved, or active, in your reading.

Read this excerpt from *The Gold Cadillac*. As you read, make notes about aspects of the story that remind you of your own life. Write "Me" in the margin when something reminds you of yourself. If you are reminded of someone else in your life, make notes like "My mother" or "My brother."

← Response notes

I do too

from *The Gold Cadillac* by Mildred D. Taylor

Though my mother didn't like the Cadillac, everybody else in the neighborhood certainly did. That meant quite a few folks too, since we lived on a very busy block. On one corner was a grocery store, a cleaner's, and a gas station. Across the street was a beauty shop and a fish market, and down the street was a bar, another grocery store, the Dixie Theater, the café, and a drugstore. There were always people strolling to or from one of these places and because our house was right in the middle of the block just about everybody had to pass our house and the gold Cadillac. Sometimes people took in the Cadillac as they walked, their heads turning for a longer look as they passed. Then there were people who just outright stopped and took a good look before continuing on their way. I was proud to say that car belonged to my family. I felt mighty important as people called to me as I ran down the street. "'Ey, 'lois! How's that Cadillac, girl? Riding fine?" I told my mother how much everybody liked that car. She was not impressed and made no comment.

Since just about everybody on the block knew everybody else, most folks knew that my mother wouldn't ride in the Cadillac. Because of that, my father took a lot of good-natured kidding from the men. My mother got kidded too as the women said if she didn't ride in that car, maybe some other woman would. And everybody laughed about it and began to bet on who would give in first, my mother or my father. But then my father said he was going to drive the car south into Mississippi to visit my grandparents and everybody stopped laughing.

14

from *The Gold Cadillac* by Mildred D. Taylor

Response notes

My uncles stopped.

So did my aunts.

Everybody.

"Look here, Wilbert," said one of my uncles, "it's too dangerous. It's like putting a loaded gun to your head."

"I paid good money for that car," said my father. "That gives me a right to drive it where I please. Even down to Mississippi."

My uncles argued with him and tried to talk him out of driving the car south. So did my aunts and so did the neighbors, Mr. LeRoy, Mr. Courtland, and Mr. Pondexter. They said it was a dangerous thing, a mighty dangerous thing, for a black man to drive an expensive car into the rural South.

"Not much those folks hate more'n to see a northern Negro coming down there in a fine car," said Mr. Pondexter. "They see those Ohio license plates, they'll figure you coming down uppity, trying to lord your fine car over them!"

I listened, but I didn't understand. I didn't understand why they didn't want my father to drive that car south. It was his.

"Listen to Pondexter, Wilbert!" cried another uncle. "We might've fought a war to free people overseas, but we're not free here! Man, those white folks down south'll lynch you soon's look at you. You know that!"

Wilma and I looked at each other. Neither one of us knew what *lynch* meant, but the word sent a shiver through us. We held each other's hand.

My father was silent, then he said: "All my life I've had to be heedful of what white folks thought. Well, I'm tired of that. I worked hard for everything I got. Got it honest, too. Now I got that Cadillac because I liked it and because it meant something to me that somebody like me from Mississippi could go and buy it. It's my car, I paid for it, and I'm driving it south."

My mother, who had said nothing through all this, now stood. "Then the girls and I'll be going too," she said.

"No!" said my father.

My mother only looked at him and went off to the kitchen.

My father shook his head. It seemed he didn't want us to go. My uncles looked at each other, then at my father. "You set on doing this, we'll all go," they said. "That way we can watch out for each other." My father took a moment and nodded. Then my aunts got up and went off to their kitchens too.

15

◗◆ Which of the narrator's thoughts, feelings, and experiences reminded you of your own life? Use the space below to list the ways you "connected" with *The Gold Cadillac*.

1. The neighborhood block the narrator describes reminds me of the block I live on.

➥ Write a journal entry describing one of your "connections" to *The Gold Cadillac*. Use your notes on page 16 to help you decide which connection to describe.

Comparing your own experiences to those in the story is one way to become involved with the selection.

Three
Language and Craft

Author's craft is like a bowl of fruit salad. The words the author uses are the different pieces of fruit in the salad. If you choose fancy, exotic fruits for your salad—kiwi, Asian pear, and mango, for example—your salad will be exotic. If an author chooses fancy words—words like *mesmerize*, *concomitant*, and *universal*—the writing will have a sophisticated feel. But there's more to author's craft than just vocabulary. A writer can't just toss a bunch of words into a paragraph and hope for the best. The words need to be carefully arranged. Author's craft is also about sentences, structure, and style.

➊➤ Use the chart to compare Taylor's craft in the excerpts from *The Gold Cadillac* and *Roll of Thunder, Hear My Cry*. Review the notes you made while reading the selections before you begin work on your chart.

Taylor's Craft	In *The Gold Cadillac*	In *Roll of Thunder, Hear My Cry*
Are there "fancy" words? Give examples.		
Are there words that create a picture? Give examples.		
How does the selection feel? (for example: happy, sad, thoughtful)		
What words would you use to describe Taylor's writing? (for example: descriptive, lots of dialogue, very detailed)		

Imagine you've been asked to make a presentation about how Mildred D. Taylor uses language. Use the index cards below to make some notes about what you will say. Base your notes on the information in your chart and your response notes.

How Mildred Taylor Uses Language

Active readers pay attention to the words authors use and the way they use them.

Every author has his or her own viewpoint or perspective. An **author's perspective** is shaped by his or her experiences, education, dreams, feelings, and so on. If you understand an author's perspective, you can understand why the author includes certain events and **details**.

What perspective does Mildred Taylor offer her readers? What does she bring to her writing that is hers and hers alone? In an interview, Taylor described her perspective this way:

"In *Roll of Thunder, Hear My Cry* (Dial 1976), I included the teachings of my own childhood, the values and principles by which I and so many other Black children were reared, for I wanted to show a different kind of Black world from the one so often seen. I wanted to show a family united in love and self-respect, and parents, strong and sensitive, attempting to guide their children successfully, without harming their spirits, through the hazardous maze of living in a discriminatory society.

I also wanted to show the Black person as heroic. In my own school days, a class devoted to the history of Black people in the United States always caused me painful embarrassment. This would not have been so if that history had been presented truly, showing the accomplishments of the Black race both in Africa and in this hemisphere. . . ."

Think about Taylor's perspective as you read this passage from her novel, *The Friendship.* In this book, Taylor tells the story of Mr. Tom Bee, an African American man who is not afraid to stand up for his rights. At this point in the novel, Tom refuses to back down when he is told to call John, a white man, "Mister." Because Tom Bee is "disrespectful," John shoots him.

← Response notes ↘

from ***The Friendship*** by Mildred D. Taylor

Mr. Tom Bee sat in silence staring at the bloody leg. "Tom, ya hear me?"

Now, slowly, Mr. Tom Bee raised his head and looked up at John Wallace. "Oh, yeah, I hears ya all right. I hears ya. But let me tell you somethin', John. Ya was John t' me when I saved your sorry life and you give me your word you was always gonna be John t' me long as I lived. So's ya might's well go 'head and kill me cause that's what ya gon' be, John. Ya hear me, John? Till the judgment day. Till the earth opens itself up and the fires-a hell come takes yo' ingrateful soul! Ya hear me, John? Ya hear me? *John! John! John!* Till the judgment day! *John!*"

With that he raised himself to one elbow and began to drag himself down the road. The boys and I, candy canes in hand, stood motionless. We watched Mr. John Wallace to see if he would raise the shotgun again. Jeremy, the candy cane in his

from *The Friendship* by Mildred D. Taylor

Response notes ↘

pocket, watched too. We all waited for the second click of the shotgun. But only the cries of Mr. Tom Bee as he inched his way along the road ripped the silence. *"John! John! John!"* he cried over and over again. "Ya hear me, John? Till the judgment day! John! *John! JOHN!"*

There was no other sound.

●✦ How does Taylor show "the Black person as heroic" in this passage?

....

....

....

●✦ Now complete the "Perspectives" chart.

TAYLOR'S PERSPECTIVE

	shows "the Black person as heroic . . ."	shows "a family united in love . . ."	shows "parents, strong and sensitive . . ."
In *The Friendship*	Yes! Tom Bee is a hero because he stands up for himself.	no family here	no parents here
In *The Gold Cadillac*			
In *Roll of Thunder, Hear My Cry*			
In "Author's Note"			

21

Recognizing author's perspective helps you understand why an author includes certain details and events.

Five Focus on the Writer

Knowing about an author's life helps you understand both the author's writing *and* perspective. Writers often write what they know. They write about the experiences they've had, the people they've met, and the places they've visited. Of course, this doesn't mean that every book is an **autobiography** (an author's account of his or her life). Usually writers borrow only bits and pieces from their own lives.

As you read the following interview, watch for connections between Taylor's life and her fiction. Circle any people, places, or events that Taylor "borrowed" for her stories.

← Response notes

The Gold
Cadillac

from an interview with Mildred D. Taylor

"From as far back as I can remember my father taught me a different history from the one I learned in school. By the fireside in our Ohio home and in Mississippi, where I was born and where my father's family had lived since the days of slavery, I had heard about our past. It was not an organized history beginning in a certain year, but one told through stories about great-grandparents and aunts and uncles and others that stretched back through the years of slavery and beyond. It was a history of ordinary people. Some brave, some not so brave, but basically people who had done nothing more spectacular than survive in a society designed for their destruction. Some of the stories my father had learned from his parents and grandparents as they had learned from theirs; others he told first-hand, having been involved in the incidents himself. There was often humor in his stories, sometimes pathos, and frequently tragedy; but always the people were graced with a simple dignity that elevated them from the ordinary to the heroic.

"Those colorful vignettes stirred the romantic in me. I was fascinated by the stories, not only because of what they said or because they were about my family, but because of the manner in which my father told them. I began to imagine myself as storyteller, making people laugh at their own human foibles or nod their heads with pride about some stunning feat of heroism. But I was a shy and quiet child, so I turned to creating stories for myself instead, carving elaborate daydreams in my mind.

"I do not know how old I was when the daydreams became more than that, and I decided to write them down, but by the time I entered high school, I was confident that I would one day be a writer. I still wonder at myself for feeling so confident since I had never particularly liked to write, nor was I exceptionally good at it. But once I had made up my mind to write, I had no doubts about doing it. It was just something

22

Response notes

that would one day be. I had always been taught that I could achieve anything I set my mind to. Still a number of years were to lapse before this setting of my mind actually resulted in the publication of any of my stories.

"In those intervening years spent studying, traveling, and living in Africa, and working with the Black student movement, I would find myself turning again and again to the stories I had heard in my childhood. One story in particular kept nagging at me, a story my father had once told me about the cutting of some beloved trees on our family land. I attempted to write it from the grandmother's point of view without success. Gradually as I struggled, new twists to the story began to emerge. At last I decided to tell it through the eyes of Cassie Logan, a spirited eight year old."

●◆ Look back at the selections you read in this unit. Use a colored pencil or marker to highlight the places where you see shades of Taylor's life. Then explain the connection in the chart below.

Story	Connection to Taylor's Life
The Gold Cadillac	I know that the narrator and her family live in Ohio because the gold Cadillac has Ohio plates. Taylor lived in Ohio when she was a child.

23

Imagine you are introducing Mildred D. Taylor—the writer and the person—to someone who has never heard of her. Include information both about Taylor's writing *and* her life in your introduction.

Mildred D. Taylor

Knowing about an author's life can help you better understand his or her writing.

Essentials of Reading

We all have opinions about what we read. Some people like to read historical fiction; others would rather read a good fantasy. Before you can decide whether or not you like what you're reading, you need to be sure that you *understand* what you're reading. After all, it's hard to enjoy something if you don't understand it.

In this unit, you'll learn some techniques that will help you better understand what you read. As you read and reflect on different types of literature, you'll practice making predictions, drawing inferences, understanding the main idea, and identifying the author's purpose.

Thinking with the Writer

Active readers know that making **predictions** is an important part of
reading. Most of the predictions we make as we read involve what might
happen next in the **plot** (the action) of a story. Read the first part of Ray
Bradbury's short story "All Summer in a Day." As you read, make
predictions in the response notes about what you think might happen next.

"All Summer in a Day" by Ray Bradbury

"Ready?"

"Ready."

"Now?"

"Soon."

"Do the scientists really know? Will it happen today, will it?"

"Look, look; see for yourself!"

The children pressed to each other like so many roses, so
many weeds, intermixed, peering out for a look at the hidden
sun.

It rained.

It had been raining for seven years; thousands upon
thousands of days compounded and filled from one end to the
other with rain, with the drum and gush of water, with the
sweet crystal fall of showers and the concussion of storms so
heavy they were tidal waves come over the islands. A
thousand forests had been crushed under the rain and grown
up a thousand times to be crushed again. And this was the
way life was forever on the planet Venus, and this was the
schoolroom of the children of the rocket men and women who
had come to a raining world to set up civilization and live out
their lives.

"It's stopping, it's stopping!"

"Yes, yes!"

Margot stood apart from them, from these children who
could never remember a time when there wasn't rain and rain
and rain. They were all nine years old, and if there had been a
day, seven years ago, when the sun came out for an hour and
showed its face to the stunned world, they could not recall.
Sometimes, at night, she heard them stir, in remembrance, and
she knew they were dreaming and remembering gold or a
yellow crayon or a coin large enough to buy the world with.
She knew that they thought they remembered a warmness,
like a blushing in the face, in the body, in the arms and legs
and trembling hands. But then they always awoke to the
tatting drum, the endless shaking down of clear bead necklaces

"All Summer in a Day" by Ray Bradbury

upon the roof, the walk, the gardens, the forests, and their dreams were gone.

All day yesterday they had read in class about the sun, about how like a lemon it was, and how hot. And they had written small stories or essays or poems about it:

I think the sun is a flower,
That blooms for just one hour.

That was Margot's poem, read in a quiet voice in the still classroom while the rain was falling outside.

"Aw, you didn't write that!" protested one of the boys.

"I did," said Margot. "I *did.*"

"William!" said the teacher.

But that was yesterday. Now the rain was slackening, and the children were crushed in the great thick windows.

"Where's teacher?"

"She'll be back."

"She'd better hurry, we'll miss it!"

They turned on themselves, like a feverish wheel, all tumbling spokes.

Margot stood alone. She was a very frail girl who looked as if she had been lost in the rain for years and the rain had washed out the blue from her eyes and the red from her mouth and the yellow from her hair. She was an old photograph dusted from an album, whitened away, and if she spoke at all her voice would be a ghost. Now she stood, separate, staring at the rain and the loud wet world beyond the huge glass.

"What are *you* looking at?" said William.

Margot said nothing.

"Speak when you're spoken to." He gave her a shove. But she did not move; rather she let herself be moved only by him and nothing else.

They edged away from her, they would not look at her. She felt them go away. And this was because she would play no games with them in the echoing tunnels of the underground city. If they tagged her and ran, she stood blinking after them and did not follow. When the class sang songs about happiness and life and games, her lips barely moved. Only when they sang about the sun and the summer did her lips move as she watched the drenched windows.

And then, of course, the biggest crime of all was that she had come here only five years ago from Earth, and she remembered the sun and the way the sun was and the sky was when she was four, in Ohio. And they, they had been on Venus all their lives, and they had been only two years old when last the sun came out and had long since forgotten the color and

27

"All Summer in a Day" by Ray Bradbury

heat of it and the way it really was. But Margot remembered.

"It's like a penny," she said once, eyes closed.

"No, it's not!" the children cried.

"It's like a fire," she said, "in the stove."

"You're lying; you don't remember!" cried the children.

But she remembered and stood quietly apart from all of them and watched the patterning windows. And once, a month ago, she had refused to shower in the school shower rooms, had clutched her hands to her ears and over her head, screaming the water mustn't touch her head. So after that, dimly, dimly, she sensed it; she was different and they knew her difference and kept away.

STOP AND PREDICT

● What do you think will happen next? Why? Use your response notes to help you explain your prediction.

....

....

....

● Based on your prediction, write a paragraph or two that continues the story as if you were the author.

....

....

....

....

....

....

....

Making predictions about the plot helps you read actively.

Two
Reading Between the Lines

An **inference** is any reasonable guess that you can make based on the evidence or information provided. How do you make inferences? Begin by thinking about the information the author has given you. For example, you might infer that Margot is a quiet, lonely girl from the way Bradbury describes her.

Read the next part of "All Summer in a Day." Circle or highlight information about Margot and the other characters. Use your response notes to jot down any inferences you make.

"All Summer in a Day" (continued) by Ray Bradbury

Response notes

There was talk that her father and mother were taking her back to Earth next year; it seemed vital to her that they do so, though it would mean the loss of thousands of dollars to her family. And so, the children hated her for all these reasons, of big and little consequence. They hated her pale, snow face, her waiting silence, her thinness, and her possible future.

"Get away!" The boy gave her another push. "What're you waiting for?"

Then, for the first time, she turned and looked at him. And what she was waiting for was in her eyes.

"Well, don't wait around here!" cried the boy, savagely. "You won't see nothing!"

Her lips moved.

"Nothing!" he cried. "It was all a joke, wasn't it?" He turned to the other children. "Nothing's happening today. *Is* it?"

They all blinked at him and then, understanding, laughed and shook their heads.

"Oh, but," Margot whispered, her eyes helpless. "But this is the day, the scientists predict, they say, they *know*, the sun . . ."

"All a joke!" said the boy and seized her roughly. "Hey, everyone, let's put her in a closet before teacher comes!"

"No," said Margot, falling back.

They surged about her, caught her up and bore her, protesting, and then pleading, and then crying, back into a tunnel, a room, a closet, where they slammed and locked the door. They stood looking at the door and saw it tremble from her beating and throwing herself against it. They heard her muffled cries. Then, smiling, they turned and went out and back down the tunnel, just as the teacher arrived.

"Ready, children?" She glanced at her watch.

"Yes!" said everyone.

"Are we all here?"

"Yes!"

The rain slackened still more.

They crowded to the huge door.

"All Summer in a Day" (continued) by Ray Bradbury

The rain stopped.

It was as if, in the midst of a film concerning an avalanche, a tornado, a hurricane, a volcanic eruption, something had, first, gone wrong with the sound apparatus, thus muffling and finally cutting off all noise, all of the blasts and repercussions and thunders, and then, second, ripped the film from the projector and inserted in its place a peaceful tropical slide which did not move or tremor. The world ground to a standstill. The silence was so immense and unbelievable that you felt your ears had been stuffed or you had lost your hearing altogether. The children put their hands to their ears. They stood apart. The door slid back and the smell of the silent, waiting world came in to them.

The sun came out.

It was the color of flaming bronze and it was very large. And the sky around it was a blazing blue tile color. And the jungle burned with sunlight as the children, released from their spell, rushed out, yelling, into the springtime.

"Now, don't go too far," called the teacher after them. "You've only one hour, you know. You wouldn't want to get caught out!"

But they were running and turning their faces up to the sky and feeling the sun on their cheeks like a warm iron; they were taking off their jackets and letting the sun burn their arms.

"Oh, it's better than sun lamps, isn't it?"

"Much, much better!"

They stopped running and stood in the great jungle that covered Venus, that grew and never stopped growing, tumultuously, even as you watched it. It was a nest of octopuses, clustering up great arms of fleshlike weed, wavering, flowering in this brief spring. It was the color of rubber and ash, this jungle, from the many years without sun. It was the color of stones and white cheeses and ink, and it was the color of the moon.

The children lay out, laughing, on the jungle mattress, and heard it sigh and squeak under them, resilient and alive. They ran among the trees, they slipped and fell, they pushed each other, they played hide-and-seek and tag; but most of all they squinted at the sun until tears ran down their faces, they put their hands up to that yellowness and that amazing blueness and they breathed of the fresh, fresh air and listened and listened to the silence which suspended them in a blessed sea of no sound and no motion. They looked at everything and savored everything. Then, wildly, like animals escaped from their caves, they ran and ran in shouting circles. They ran for an hour and did not stop running.

"All Summer in a Day" (continued) by Ray Bradbury

Response notes

And then—
In the midst of their running one of the girls wailed.
Everyone stopped.
The girl, standing in the open, held out her hand.
"Oh, look, look," she said trembling.
They came slowly to look at her opened palm.
In the center of it, cupped and huge, was a single raindrop.
She began to cry, looking at it.
They glanced quickly at the sky.
"Oh. Oh."

A few cold drops fell on their noses and their cheeks and their mouths. The sun faded behind a stir of mist. A wind blew cool around them. They turned and started to walk back toward the underground house, their hands at their sides, their smiles vanishing away.

A boom of thunder startled them and like leaves before a new hurricane, they tumbled upon each other and ran. Lightning struck ten miles away, five miles away, a mile, a half mile. The sky darkened into midnight in a flash.

They stood in the doorway of the underground for a moment until it was raining hard. Then they closed the door and heard the gigantic sound of the rain falling in tons and avalanches, everywhere and forever.

"Will it be seven more years?"
"Yes. Seven."
Then one of them gave a little cry.
"Margot!"
"What?"
"She's still in the closet where we locked her."
"Margot."

They stood as if someone had driven them, like so many stakes, into the floor. They looked at each other and then looked away. They glanced out at the world that was raining now and raining and raining steadily. They could not meet each other's glances. Their faces were solemn and pale. They looked at their hands and feet, their faces down.

"Margot."
One of the girls said, "Well . . . ?"
No one moved.
"Go on," whispered the girl.

They walked slowly down the hall in the sound of cold rain. They turned through the doorway to the room in the sound of the storm and thunder, lightning on their faces, blue and terrible. They walked over to the closet door slowly and stood by it.

Behind the closet door was only silence.
They unlocked the door, even more slowly, and let Margot out.

31

●◆First, check the predictions you made in Lesson One. Did your predictions match what actually happened in the story? Did making predictions help you get involved in the story? Explain.

....

....

....

●◆Now return to the story. Underline any information you can find about William and Margot. Then imagine you are one of these characters. Write a journal entry explaining your reaction to the day's events. Use the inferences you made while reading to help you decide what the character would write.

32

....

....

....

....

....

....

....

....

....

....

....

....

Making inferences about the characters can help deepen your understanding of a story.

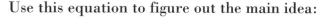

Three
Managing the Main Idea

The **main idea** is the central focus of a piece of writing. It is the "big idea" the author wants readers to understand. You can usually discover the main idea by first identifying the *subject* of the writing (the person, place, or thing the author is writing about), and then figuring out what the author has to say about the subject.

Use this equation to figure out the main idea:

[subject] + [what the author says about the subject] = the main idea

Read this essay by Mickey Roberts. As you read, make notes about the subject of the piece. Underline words and phrases that provide clues about the main idea.

"It's All in How You Say It" by Mickey Roberts

Response notes

Ever since I was a young girl in school, I've been aware of what the school textbooks say about Indians. I am an Indian and, naturally, am interested in what the school teaches about natives of this land.

One day in the grammar school I attended, I read that a delicacy of American Indian people was dried fish, which, according to the textbook, tasted "like an old shoe, or was like chewing on dried leather." To this day I can remember my utter dismay at reading these words. We called this wind-dried fish "leet-schus," and to us, it was our favorite delicacy and, indeed, did not taste like shoe leather. It took many hours of long and hard work to cure the fish in just this particular fashion. Early fur traders and other non-Indians must have agreed, for they often used this food for subsistence as they traveled around isolated areas.

I brought the textbook home to show it to my father, leader of my tribe at the time. My father was the youngest son of one of the last chiefs of the Nooksack Indian Tribe of Whatcom County in the state of Washington. On this particular day, he told me in his wise and humble manner that the outside world did not always understand Indian people, and that I should not let it hinder me from learning the good parts of my education.

Since those early years I have learned we were much better off with our own delicacies, which did not rot our teeth and bring about the various dietary problems that plague Indian people in modern times. I was about eight years old when this incident happened and it did much to sharpen my desire to pinpoint terminology in books used to describe American Indian people, books which are, most often, not very complimentary.

At a later time in my life, I had brought a group of Indian

"It's All in How You Say It" by Mickey Roberts

people to the county fairgrounds to put up a booth to sell Indian-made arts and crafts. My group was excited about the prospect of making some money selling genuine Indian artifacts. We thanked the man who showed us our booth and told him it was nice of him to remember the people of the Indian community. The man expanded a little and remarked that he liked Indian people. "In fact," he went on to state, "we are bringing some professional Indians to do the show!"

As we stood there in shock, listening to this uninformed outsider, I looked at my dear Indian companion, an eighty-year-old woman who could well remember the great chiefs of the tribe who once owned all the land of this county before the white man came bringing "civilization," which included diseases and pollution. My friend said not a word, but took the hurt as Indian people have done for many years, realizing outsiders are very often tactless and unthinking.

Of course, we all knew that the "professional Indians" were not Indians at all, but dressed in leather and dancing their own dances. And, anyway, how does one become a "professional Indian"?

I remembered my father's words of so long ago and said to my friend as my father had said to me, "They just don't understand Indian people."

34

●◆ Complete a main idea equation for "It's All in How You Say It."

+	=
(subject)	(what the author says about subject)	(main idea)

Now return to the essay. Find the sentence that best expresses the author's main idea and underline it.

●◆ In "It's All in How You Say It," Mickey Roberts explains how she feels when she and her people are misunderstood. Write about a time you felt misunderstood. Explain what happened and how you felt. Before you begin, fill in a "main idea" equation to help you identify the main idea of your writing.

+	=
(subject)	(what I will say about subject)	(main idea)

➥ Use the space below to write about a time you felt misunderstood. Use your "main idea" equation to help focus your writing.

35

Recognizing the main idea helps you understand what the author has to say about a subject.

Four Author's Purpose

Authors write for a variety of reasons, including to entertain, to inform or teach, to persuade or argue, and to express personal thoughts and feelings. Authors often write in different genres for different purposes. Sometimes an author will have more than one purpose. For example, in a newspaper article, the author may want to inform *and* persuade.

As you read "Holiday Dinner," make notes about the **author's purpose**. Write "entertain," "inform," "persuade," or "express thoughts and feelings" in the margins of the poem where appropriate.

Response notes

Holiday Dinner
Felice Holman

We're sitting at table,
all of us,
sighing with joy
of too much good food
and Gramps says,
"When I was a boy . . ."
and we all snore
because we know
we've heard it before—
about how he had to
patch his shoes and
chop the wood
and catch the goose
and . . .
But we listen
(and even the snore is
part of it, surely)
because if we didn't
our hearts
would miss it sorely.

◆ What do you think of the poem?

●◆ What do you think Holman's purpose is? Use your response notes to support your opinion.

....

....

....

....

....

●◆ Do you think a poem fits this purpose? Discuss whether other types of writing—such as a short story, a letter, or a biography—would have suited Holman's purposes as well.

....

....

....

....

....

....

....

....

....

....

....

The author's purpose helps him or her decide what kind of piece to write.

Five Reflecting on Reading

Reflecting helps readers get a better understanding of what they've read. Reflecting involves thinking about the writing in terms of your own life. Ask yourself, "What have I learned from reading this selection?"

➥ Reflect on "Holiday Dinner." Write a paragraph explaining what you learned from Holman's poem.

....

....

....

....

➥ Think about your own experiences with holiday dinners. How are they similar to the one Holman describes? How are they different? Reflect on your connections to the poem in the space below.

....

....

....

....

....

....

....

....

....

Reflection gives you a better understanding of a selection and your own responses to it.

39

Essentials of Story

Think of a recipe for your favorite dessert. What happens if you forget an ingredient? If you forget the flour, the cake is gooey. If you forget the chocolate chips, the cookies are bland. The same thing happens with a story. If a writer skips a story ingredient, the story doesn't work.

In this unit, you'll learn about the five basic ingredients of a story:

- setting
- character
- point of view
- plot
- theme

You'll also discover how a "master writer" (like a "master chef") can blend these ingredients together to make a story that is truly delicious.

One — A Story's Setting

Setting is the time and place of a story (<u>when</u> and <u>where</u> the action occurs). Sometimes the setting is very important. (Think about your favorite science fiction story. Could it have taken place anywhere else but on Planet X?) In other stories, you might not notice the setting, although it's there if you look for it.

Read this short passage from Natalie Babbitt's novel *The Search for Delicious*. Underline or circle any words or phrases that relate to *time*. Use your response notes to explain how time is important.

response notes

from *The Search for Delicious* by Natalie Babbitt

There was a time once when the earth was still very young, a time some call the oldest days. This was long before there were any people about to dig parts of it up and cut parts of it off. People came along much later, building their towns and castles (which nearly always fell down after a while) and plaguing each other with quarrels and supper parties. The creatures who lived on the earth in that early time stayed each in his own place and kept it beautiful. There were dwarfs in the mountains, woldwellers in the forests, mermaids in the lakes, and, of course, winds in the air.

Next read this passage from Madeleine L'Engle's fantasy, *A Wrinkle in Time*. Underline or circle any words or phrases that relate to *place*.

from *A Wrinkle in Time* by Madeleine L'Engle

"But *where* am I?" Meg asked breathlessly, relieved to hear that her voice was now coming out of her in more or less a normal way.

She looked around rather wildly. They were standing in a sunlit field, and the air about them was moving with the delicious fragrance that comes only on the rarest of spring days when the sun's touch is gentle and the apple blossoms are just beginning to unfold. She pushed her glasses up on her nose to reassure herself that what she was seeing was real.

They had left the silver glint of a biting autumn evening; and now around them everything was golden with light. The grasses of the field were a tender new green, and scattered about were tiny, multicolored flowers. Meg turned slowly to face a mountain reaching so high into the sky that its peak was lost in a crown of puffy white clouds. From the trees at the base of the mountain came a sudden singing of birds. There was an air of such ineffable peace and joy all around her that her heart's wild thumping slowed.

●◆Which of the two settings creates the most vivid impression? Why?

●◆Now imagine you have been asked to create the *backdrop* (or background scene) for your school's production of one of these selections. Choose your favorite. Then use colored pencils, markers, crayons, or pastels to create your scene.

41

A detailed setting helps readers visualize where the events of a story take place.

TWO A Story's Characters

Every story needs **characters**—people or animals or even imaginary creatures. But it's not enough to insert a character or two into a story and leave it at that. Characters need to be interesting. They also need to be memorable. Some characters are memorable because of the way they look or act or talk. Sometimes it's what the characters think and feel that makes them so interesting.

Read this excerpt from the novel *Danny the Champion of the World*. As you read, think about the narrator's attitude toward the character he describes. According to the narrator, what makes his father special? Use the margins of your *Daybook* to make notes about how the narrator's father looks, acts, and feels.

←—Response notes—→

from *Danny the Champion of the World* by Roald Dahl

You might think, if you didn't know him well, that he was a stern and serious man. He wasn't. He was actually a wildly funny person. What made him appear so serious was the fact that he never smiled with his mouth. He did it all with his eyes. He had brilliant blue eyes and when he thought of something funny, his eyes would flash and, if you looked carefully, you could actually see a tiny little golden spark dancing in the middle of each eye. But the mouth never moved.

I was glad my father was an eye-smiler. It meant he never gave me a fake smile because it's impossible to make your eyes twinkle if you aren't feeling twinkly yourself. A mouth-smile is different. You can fake a mouth-smile any time you want, simply by moving your lips. I've also learned that a real mouth-smile always has an eye-smile to go with it. So watch out, I say, when someone smiles at you with his mouth but his eyes stay the same. It's sure to be a phony.

My father was not what you would call an educated man. I doubt he had read twenty books in his life. But he was a marvelous storyteller. He used to make up a bedtime story for me every single night, and the best ones were turned into serials and went on for many nights running.

One of them, which must have gone on for at least fifty nights, was about an enormous fellow called "The Big Friendly Giant," or "The BFG" for short. The BFG was three times as tall as an ordinary man and his hands were as big as wheelbarrows. He lived in a vast underground cavern not far from our filling station and he only came out into the open when it was dark. Inside the cavern he had a powder factory where he made more than one hundred different kinds of magic powder.

from **Danny the Champion of the World** by Roald Dahl

"The Big Friendly Giant makes his magic powders out of the dreams that children dream when they are asleep," he said.

"How?" I asked. "Tell me how, dad."

"Dreams, my love, are very mysterious things. They float around in the night air like little clouds, searching for sleeping people."

"Can you see them?" I asked.

"Nobody can see them."

"Then how does The Big Friendly Giant catch them?"

"Ah," my father said, "that is the interesting part. A dream, you see, as it goes drifting through the night air, makes a tiny little buzzing-humming sound, a sound so soft and low it is impossible for ordinary people to hear it. But The BFG can hear it easily. His sense of hearing is absolutely fantastic."

I loved the intent look on my father's face when he was telling a story. His face was pale and still and distant, unconscious of everything around him.

"The BFG," he said, "can hear the tread of a ladybug's footsteps as she walks across a leaf. He can hear the whisperings of ants as they scurry around in the soil talking to one another. He can hear the sudden shrill cry of pain a tree gives out when a woodman cuts into it with an ax. Ah yes, my darling, there is a whole world of sound around us that we cannot hear because our ears are simply not sensitive enough."

"What happens when he catches the dreams?" I asked.

"He imprisons them in glass bottles and screws the tops down tight," my father said. "He has thousands of these bottles in his cave."

"Does he catch bad dreams as well as good ones?"

"Yes," my father said. "He catches both. But he only uses the good ones in his powders."

"What does he do with the bad ones?"

"He explodes them."

It is impossible to tell you how much I loved my father. When he was sitting close to me on my bunk I would reach out and slide my hand into his, and then he would fold his long fingers around my fist, holding it tight.

◆◆Characters' words and actions often reveal their feelings. What do Danny's father's words and actions reveal about his feelings? Explain.

43

A word picture is a picture drawn with words instead of lines and curves. For example, here is a word picture someone might make to represent a grandmother:

●◆Make a word picture of Danny's father. First, return to the excerpt from *Danny the Champion of the World*. Circle words or phrases that describe Danny's father. Then make a list of words that describe him. Use the list to draw your word picture.

44

Noticing details about characters can help you "get into" a story.

Three
A Story's Point of View

The third ingredient for a successful story is **point of view**—the angle from which a story is told. If the point of view changes, so does the story. Active readers know that understanding point of view is as easy as deciding who the **narrator** (or storyteller) is.

Read another excerpt from *Danny the Champion of the World.* As you read, highlight or circle any information you find about the narrator. Use the response notes to make observations about what point of view the author is using.

from **Danny the Champion of the World** by Roald Dahl

Response notes

And so life went on. The world I lived in consisted only of the filling station, the workshop, the caravan, the school, and of course the woods and meadows and streams in the countryside around. But I was never bored. It was impossible to be bored in my father's company. He was too sparky a man for that. Plots and plans and new ideas came flying off him like sparks from a grindstone.

"There's a good wind today," he said one Saturday morning. "Just right for flying a kite. Let's make a kite, Danny."

So we made a kite. He showed me how to splice four thin sticks together in the shape of a star, with two more sticks across the middle to brace it. Then we cut up an old blue shirt of his and stretched the material across the framework of the kite. We added a long tail made of thread, with little leftover pieces of the shirt tied at intervals along it. We found a ball of string in the workshop, and he showed me how to attach the string to the framework so that the kite would be properly balanced in flight.

Together we walked to the top of the hill behind the filling station to release the kite. I found it hard to believe that this object, made only from a few sticks and a piece of old shirt, would actually fly. I held the string while my father held the kite, and the moment he let it go, it caught the wind and soared upward like a huge blue bird.

"Let out some more, Danny!" he cried. "Go on! As much as you like!"

Higher and higher soared the kite. Soon it was just a small blue dot dancing in the sky miles above my head, and it was thrilling to stand there holding on to something that was so far away and so very much alive. This faraway thing was tugging and struggling on the end of the line like a big fish.

"Let's walk it back to the caravan," my father said.

So we walked down the hill again with me holding the string and the kite still pulling fiercely on the other end. When we

45

from **Danny the Champion of the World** by Roald Dahl

came to the caravan we were careful not to get the string tangled in the apple tree and we brought it all the way around to the front steps.

"Tie it to the steps," my father said.

"Will it still stay up?" I asked.

"It will if the wind doesn't drop," he said.

The wind didn't drop. And I will tell you something amazing. That kite stayed up there all through the night, and at breakfast time next morning the small blue dot was still dancing and swooping in the sky. After breakfast I hauled it down and hung it carefully against a wall in the workshop for another day.

How would the scene the narrator describes be different if it were told from the father's point of view? Use what you know about Danny and his father to rewrite the kite-flying scene from the father's point of view. Be as creative as you like, but make sure you give readers an adult angle on the events.

Point of view is the angle from which a story is told. If the point of view changes, so does the story.

Four
A Story's Plot

Plot is the action of a story: it's what *happens*. A plot usually has five parts: exposition, rising action, climax, falling action, and resolution.

Climax

Rising Action

Falling Action

Exposition

Resolution

47

The **exposition** is the part of a story (usually the beginning) that explains the background and setting and introduces the characters of the story.

The **rising action** is the central part of a story during which various problems arise, leading up to the climax.

The **climax** is the highest point (turning point) in the action of a story. The climax causes the action of the story to change.

The **falling action** follows the climax or turning point. It contains the action or dialogue necessary to lead the story to a resolution or ending.

The **resolution** is the end of a story—that part in which the problems are solved or the story gets "wrapped up."

As you read "A Game of Catch," by Richard Wilbur, think about the plot of the story. When you see one of the plot parts, circle the section and identify which part of the plot you think it is: exposition, rising action, climax, falling action, or resolution.

"A Game of Catch" by Richard Wilbur

←Response notes→

Monk and Glennie were playing catch on the side lawn of the firehouse when Scho caught sight of them. They were good at it, for seventh-graders, as anyone could see right away. Monk, wearing a catcher's mitt, would lean easily sidewise and back, with one leg lifted and his throwing hand almost down to the grass, and then lob the white ball straight up into the sunlight. Glennie would shield his eyes with his left hand and, just as the ball fell past him, snag it with a little dart of his glove. Then he would burn the ball straight toward Monk, and it would spank into the round mitt and sit, like a still-life apple on a plate, until Monk flipped it over into his right hand and, with a negligent flick of his hanging arm, gave Glennie a fast grounder.

They were going on and on like that, in a kind of slow, mannered, luxurious dance in the sun, their faces perfectly blank and entranced, when Glennie noticed Scho dawdling along the other side of the street and called hello to him. Scho crossed over and stood at the front edge of the lawn, near an apple tree, watching.

"Got your glove?" asked Glennie after a time. Scho obviously hadn't.

"You could give me some easy grounders," said Scho. "But don't burn 'em."

"All right," Glennie said. He moved off a little, so the three of them formed a triangle, and they passed the ball around for about five minutes, Monk tossing easy grounders to Scho, Scho throwing to Glennie, and Glennie burning them in to Monk. After a while, Monk began to throw them back to Glennie once or twice before he let Scho have his grounder, and finally Monk gave Scho a fast, bumpy grounder that hopped over his shoulder and went into the brake on the other side of the street.

"Not so hard," called Scho as he ran across to get it.

"You should've had it," Monk shouted.

It took Scho a little while to find the ball among the ferns and dead leaves, and when he saw it, he grabbed it up and threw it toward Glennie. It struck the trunk of the apple tree,

48

"A Game of Catch" by Richard Wilbur

Response notes

bounced back at an angle, and rolled steadily and stupidly onto the cement apron in front of the firehouse, where one of the trucks was parked. Scho ran hard and stopped it just before it rolled under the truck, and this time he carried it back to his former position on the lawn and threw it carefully to Glennie.

"I got an idea," said Glennie. "Why don't Monk and I catch for five minutes more, and then you can borrow one of our gloves?"

"That's all right with me," said Monk. He socked his fist into his mitt, and Glennie burned one in.

"All right," Scho said, and went over and sat under the tree. There in the shade he watched them resume their skillful play. They threw lazily fast or lazily slow—high, low, or wide—and always handsomely, their expressions serene, changeless, and forgetful. When Monk missed a low backhand catch, he walked indolently after the ball and, hardly even looking, flung it sidearm for an imaginary put-out. After a good while of this, Scho said, "Isn't it five minutes yet?"

"One minute to go," said Monk, with a fraction of a grin.

Scho stood up and watched the ball slap back and forth for several minutes more, and then he turned and pulled himself up into the crotch of the tree.

"Where are you going?" Monk asked.

"Just up the tree," Scho said.

"I guess he doesn't want to catch," said Monk.

Scho went up and up through the fat light-gray branches until they grew slender and bright and gave under him. He found a place where several supple branches were knit to make a dangerous chair, and sat there with his head coming out of the leaves into the sunlight. He could see the two other boys down below, the ball going back and forth between them as if they were bowling on the grass, and Glennie's crew-cut head looking like a sea urchin.

"I found a wonderful seat up here," Scho said loudly. "If I don't fall out." Monk and Glennie didn't look up or comment, and so he began jouncing gently in his chair of branches and singing "Yo-ho, heave ho" in an exaggerated way.

"Do you know what, Monk?" he announced in a few moments. "I can make you two guys do anything I want. Catch that ball, Monk! Now you catch it, Glennie!"

"I was going to catch it anyway," Monk suddenly said. "You're not making anybody do anything when they're already going to do it anyway."

"I made you say what you just said," Scho replied joyfully.

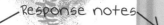

"A Game of Catch" by Richard Wilbur

"No, you didn't," said Monk, still throwing and catching but now less serenely absorbed in the game.

"That's what I wanted you to say," Scho said.

The ball bounced off the rim of Monk's mitt and plowed into a gladiolus bed beside the firehouse, and Monk ran to get it while Scho jounced in his treetop and sang, "I wanted you to miss that. Anything you do is what I wanted you to do."

"Let's quit for a minute," Glennie suggested.

"We might as well, until the peanut gallery shuts up," Monk said.

They went over and sat cross-legged in the shade of the tree. Scho looked down between his legs and saw them on the dim spotty ground, saying nothing to one another. Glennie soon began abstractedly spinning his glove between his palms; Monk pulled his nose and stared out across the lawn.

"I want you to mess around with your nose, Monk," said Scho, giggling. Monk withdrew his hand from his face.

"Do that with your glove, Glennie," Scho persisted. "Monk, I want you to pull up hunks of grass and chew on it."

Glennie looked up and saw a self-delighted, intense face staring down at him through the leaves. "Stop being a dope and come down and we'll catch for a few minutes," he said.

Scho hesitated, and then said, in a tentatively mocking voice, "That's what I wanted you to say."

"Why don't you keep quiet and stop bothering people?" Monk asked.

"I made you say that," Scho replied, softly.

"Shut up," Monk said.

"I made you say that, and I want you to be standing there looking sore. And I want you to climb up the tree! I'm making you do it!"

Monk was scrambling up through the branches, awkward in his haste, and getting snagged on twigs. His face was furious and foolish, and he kept telling Scho to shut up, shut up, shut up, while the other's exuberant and panicky voice poured down upon his head.

"*Now* you shut up or you'll be sorry," Monk said, breathing hard as he reached up and threatened to shake the cradle of slight branches in which Scho was sitting.

"I *want* —" Scho screamed as he fell. Two lower branches broke his rustling, cracking fall, but he landed on his back with a deep thud and lay still, with a strangled look on his face and his eyes clenched. Glennie knelt down and asked breathlessly, "Are you OK, Scho? Are you OK?," while Monk

50

"A Game of Catch" by Richard Wilbur

Response notes

swung down through the leaves crying that honestly he hadn't even touched him, the crazy guy just let go. Scho doubled up and turned over on his right side, and now both the other boys knelt beside him, pawing at his shoulder and begging to know how he was.

Then Scho rolled away from them and sat partly up, still struggling to get his wind but forcing a species of smile into his face.

"I'm sorry, Scho," Monk said. "I didn't mean to make you fall."

Scho's voice came out weak and gravelly, in gasps. "I meant—you to do it. You—had to. You can't do—anything—unless I want—you to."

Glennie and Monk looked helplessly at him as he sat there, breathing a bit more easily and smiling fixedly, with tears in his eyes. Then they picked up their gloves and the ball, walked over to the street, and went slowly away down the sidewalk, Monk punching his fist into the mitt, Glennie juggling the ball between glove and hand.

From under the apple tree, Scho, still bent over a little for lack of breath, croaked after them in triumph and misery, "I want you to do whatever you're going to do for the whole rest of your life!"

51

●◆ Create a "plot mountain" for "A Game of Catch." Then use the
mountain to write a brief summary of the plot.

Climax:

Falling Action:

Rising
Action: Monk climbs up the
tree after Scho.

Exposition:

Resolution:

Paying
attention to a story's action helps
you understand its plot.

Five
A Story's Theme

A story's **theme** is its central idea. It is a statement or message about life that the author wants to send to the reader. Sometimes an author will state the theme directly. Other times readers will need to make **inferences** (or reasonable guesses) about the theme from what the author says. And sometimes readers can connect a story's theme to their own lives.

➥ Reread "A Game of Catch." What do you think the author might want readers to learn from this story? Explain.

➥ Now restate your answer as a theme statement for "A Game of Catch."

One theme of "A Game of Catch" is

●◆Connect this theme to your own life. Describe an experience or situation you've had that relates to the story's theme. What did you learn from your experience?

Readers can find deeper meaning in a story by connecting the story's theme to their own lives.

Understanding Character

Sometimes reading a book or a story can be a little like solving a mystery. The author gives you a series of clues about plot, characters, and theme. It's up to you to put those clues together in order to understand why the characters think and act as they do. Most of the time you can find clues about characters by looking at five different aspects of character:

- How the character looks
- How the character acts
- What the character says
- What the character thinks and feels
- How other characters respond to the character

One A Character's Appearance

Begin your hunt for clues about **character** by finding words or phrases that describe how a character *looks*. Often a writer will tell you about a character's face or body or clothes in order to help you paint a picture in your mind. If you can **visualize** the characters, you can become involved in the story.

Read the first part of "Utzel and His Daughter Poverty." As you read, underline any descriptions of how the characters Utzel and Poverty look. You might want to use two different-colored markers. Also make notes in the margin about any words or phrases you don't understand.

response notes

"Utzel and His Daughter Poverty" by Isaac Bashevis Singer

Once there was a man named Utzel. He was very poor and even more lazy. Whenever anyone wanted to give him a job to do, his answer was always the same: "Not today."

"Why not today?" he was asked. And he always replied, "Why not tomorrow?"

Utzel lived in a cottage that had been built by his great-grandfather. The thatched roof needed mending and although the holes let the rain in, they did not let the smoke from the stove out. Toadstools grew on the crooked walls and the floor had rotted away. There had been a time when mice lived there, but now there weren't any because there was nothing for them to eat. Utzel's wife had starved to death, but before she died she had given birth to a baby girl. The name Utzel gave his daughter was very fitting. He called her Poverty.

Utzel loved to sleep and each night he went to bed with the chickens. In the morning he would complain that he was tired from so much sleeping and so he went to sleep again. When he was not sleeping, he lay on his broken-down cot, yawning and complaining. He would say to his daughter: "Other people are lucky. They have money without working. I am cursed."

Utzel was a small man, but as his daughter Poverty grew, she spread out in all directions. She was tall, broad, and heavy. At fifteen she had to lower her head to get through the doorway. Her feet were the size of a man's and puffy with fat. The villagers maintained that the lazier Utzel got, the more Poverty grew.

Utzel loved nobody, was jealous of everybody. He even spoke with envy of cats, dogs, rabbits, and all creatures who didn't have to work for a living. Yes, Utzel hated everybody and everything, but he adored his daughter. He daydreamed

56

"Utzel and His Daughter Poverty" by Isaac Bashevis Singer

RESPONSE NOTES

that a rich young man would fall in love with her, marry her, and provide for his wife and his father-in-law. But not a young man in the village showed the slightest interest in Poverty. When her father reproached the girl for not making friends and not going out with young men, Poverty would say: "How can I go out in rags and bare feet?"

One day Utzel learned that a certain charitable society in the village loaned poor people money, which they could pay back in small sums over a long period. Lazy as he was, he made a great effort—got up, dressed, and went to the office of the society. "I would like to borrow five gulden," he said to the official in charge.

"What do you intend to do with the money?" he was asked. "We only lend money for useful purposes."

"I want to have a pair of shoes made for my daughter," Utzel explained. "If Poverty has shoes, she will go out with the young people of the village and some wealthy young man will surely fall in love with her. When they get married, I will be able to pay back the five gulden."

The official thought it over. The chances of anyone falling in love with Poverty were very small. Utzel, however, looked so miserable that the official decided to give him the loan. He asked Utzel to sign a promissory note and gave him five gulden.

Utzel had tried to order a pair of shoes for his daughter a few months before. Sandler, the shoemaker, had gone so far as to take Poverty's measurements, but the shoemaker had wanted his money in advance. From the charitable society Utzel went directly to the shoemaker and asked him whether he still had Poverty's measurements.

"And supposing I do?" Sandler replied. "My price is five gulden and I still want my money in advance."

Utzel took out the five gulden and handed them to Sandler. The shoemaker opened a drawer and after some searching brought out the order for Poverty's shoes. He promised to deliver the new shoes in a week, on Friday.

●◆Look over the notes you made while reading the story. Notice that Singer describes Poverty in much greater detail than Utzel. Use the web below to list words that describe how Poverty looks.

Poverty

heavy

58

●◆Use your web to draw a sketch of Poverty here.

▬◆Now create a funny character you might include in a story of your own. Describe the character and then draw a picture of him or her.

Visualizing characters helps you become involved in a story.

Two · A Character's Actions

Y ou can also learn about a character by paying attention to what the character does. Notice whether a character's actions change over the course of a story. If this happens, ask yourself these three questions:

- In what ways does the character's behavior change?
- What caused this change in behavior?
- What clues can the changes give me about the character?

In "Utzel and His Daughter Poverty," the two main characters both change. Read the rest of Singer's story. As you read, make some notes about how the characters act. If you see them acting "out of character," put a star next to that part of the story.

← Response notes

"Utzel and His Daughter Poverty" (continued)
by Isaac Bashevis Singer

Utzel, who wanted to surprise his daughter, did not tell her about the shoes. The following Friday, as he lay on his cot yawning and complaining, there was a knock on the door and Sandler came in carrying the new shoes. When Poverty saw the shoemaker with a pair of shiny, new shoes in his hand, she cried out in joy. The shoemaker handed her the shoes and told her to try them on. But, alas, she could not get them on her puffy feet. In the months since the measurements had been taken, Poverty's feet had become even larger than they were before. Now the girl cried out in grief.

Utzel looked on in consternation. "How is it possible?" he asked. "I thought her feet stopped growing long ago."

For a while Sandler, too, stood there puzzled. Then he inquired: "Tell me, Utzel, where did you get the five gulden?" Utzel explained that he had borrowed the money from the charitable loan society and had given them a promissory note in return.

"So now you have a debt," exclaimed Sandler. "That makes you even poorer than you were a few months ago. Then you had nothing, but today you have five gulden less than nothing. And since you have grown poorer, Poverty has grown bigger and naturally her feet have grown with her. That is why the shoes don't fit. It is all clear to me now."

"What are we going to do?" Utzel asked in despair.

"There is only one way out for you," Sandler said. "Go to work. From borrowing one gets poorer and from work one gets richer. When you and your daughter work, she will have shoes that fit."

"Utzel and His Daughter Poverty" (continued)
by Isaac Bashevis Singer

Response notes

The idea of working did not appeal to either of them, but it was even worse to have new shoes and go around barefoot. Utzel and Poverty both decided that immediately after the Sabbath they would look for work.

Utzel got a job as a water carrier. Poverty became a maid. For the first time in their lives, they worked diligently. They were kept so busy that they did not even think of the new shoes until one Sabbath morning Poverty decided she'd try them on again. Lo and behold, her feet slipped easily into them. The new shoes fit.

At last Utzel and Poverty understood that all a man possesses he gains through work, and not by lying in bed and being idle. Even animals are industrious. Bees make honey, spiders spin webs, birds build nests, moles dig holes in the earth, squirrels store food for the winter. Before long Utzel got a better job. He rebuilt his house and bought some furniture. Poverty lost more weight. She had new clothes made and dressed prettily like the other girls of the village. Her looks improved too, and a young man began to court her. His name was Mahir and he was the son of a wealthy merchant. Utzel's dream of a rich son-in-law came true, but by then he no longer needed to be taken care of.

Love for his daughter had saved Utzel. In his later years he became so respected he was elected a warden of that same charitable loan society from which he had borrowed five gulden.

On the wall of his office there hung the string with which Sandler had once measured Poverty's feet, and above it the framed motto: "Whatever you can do today, don't put off till tomorrow."

61

●◆ Were you surprised by the changes that took place in Utzel and Poverty? Why or why not?

➡️ Imagine you are Utzel. You have just been elected warden of the charitable loan society. Write the speech you will give at the celebration dinner. In your speech explain:

- how and why your behavior changed
- what you learned from your experience

62

Three A Character's Speech

You can learn about a character by thinking about how a character *looks* and by watching what a character *does*. Active readers know that what a character *says* can provide you with clues as well. What can a character's speech tell you about what a character is like? Think about a character who says things like: "I hate this show" and "School's boring" and "I'm not going to a silly old party." If you "read between the lines," you might **infer** that this character is a grouch.

Read this excerpt from Paula Fox's award-winning novel, *One-Eyed Cat*. As you read, underline any **dialogue** (the talking that goes on between characters in a story) that gives you clues about the characters' personalities.

from *One-Eyed Cat* by Paula Fox

Response notes

"There's nothing wrong with a plain life," Uncle Hilary said with a little smile that seemed to say there *was* something wrong with it. "I get worn out by hotels and trains and languages I can't speak, and oh, my poor stomach, the things it has to put up with! Sheep's eyes and lung stew—"

"And tomatoes covered with sugar," interrupted Papa, laughing.

Uncle Hilary looked a little put out, Ned thought, as though he were the one supposed to make jokes. Then he said, "I just think it would do Ned a world of good. He's never been away from here."

"Would you like that?" Papa suddenly asked Ned, bending slightly so he could see Ned under the table's edge. "Uncle Hilary wants to take you on a trip during your Christmas vacation."

Ned's heart leaped. He wanted to shout, Yes! There was something in his father's voice that he hadn't understood; it made him uneasy. If he said yes, he wanted to go with Uncle Hilary, would Papa think he wanted to get away from him?

"Could you come, too?" he asked.

"Ned, you know I can't leave your mother," Papa said reproachfully.

"I must think of a place to take you that will fit exactly into ten days," Uncle Hilary said.

"Ned, do come out from under the table," Papa said with the special patience he had when he was trying not to be cross. Ned got to his feet.

Uncle Hilary's visits were always brief. It was probably best that way, Ned thought. He'd noticed that his father was often touchy when his brother-in-law was staying with them. Uncle

from *One-Eyed Cat* by Paula Fox

Hilary did like to tease Papa—the way he had about putting sugar on tomatoes.

"The Georgia Sea Islands are too far," said Uncle Hilary pensively. "But perhaps we could manage Nag's Head."

"Well, Ned?" questioned his father.

Uncle Hilary smiled at him. He looks like electricity, thought Ned and that made him grin. "I think he'd like to go," said his uncle.

"Yes, I do want to," Ned said, looking at Papa.

"Fine, then," Papa said. He looked away from Ned, out the window. "We'll have a harvest moon tonight," he said.

●❖ Based on what the characters have to say in the excerpt, which one do you find most interesting? Explain.

●◆Now fill out a "Personality Profile" about the character you chose. Use the "How Do You Know?" column to explain how you arrived at your answers.

Personality Profile of: ....

QUESTION	YOUR ANSWER	HOW DO YOU KNOW?
How old is the character?		
Is the character friendly or unfriendly?		
Is the character quiet or noisy?		
Is the character smart?		
What does the character look like?		

65

"Listening" to what a character says helps you better understand the character.

A Character's Thoughts and Feelings

A character's thoughts and feelings can affect the way a character acts. If you understand why a character is feeling a particular way, you can understand why a character *acts* in a particular way. Sometimes a character's emotions are very clear. Other times, you have to make **inferences** (or reasonable guesses) to understand how the character feels.

Read "Kim," an excerpt from Paul Fleischman's novel *Seedfolks*. As you read, circle the words that tell you how Kim is feeling.

"Kim" from *Seedfolks* by Paul Fleischman

I stood before our family altar. It was dawn. No one else in the apartment was awake. I stared at my father's photograph—his thin face stern, lips latched tight, his eyes peering permanently to the right. I was nine years old and still hoped that perhaps his eyes might move. Might notice me.

The candles and the incense sticks, lit the day before to mark his death anniversary, had burned out. The rice and meat offered him were gone. After the evening feast, past midnight, I'd been wakened by my mother's crying. My oldest sister had joined in. My own tears had then come as well, but for a different reason.

I turned from the altar, tiptoed to the kitchen, and quietly drew a spoon from a drawer. I filled my lunch thermos with water and reached into our jar of dried lima beans. Then I walked outside to the street.

The sidewalk was completely empty. It was Sunday, early in April. An icy wind teetered trash cans and turned my cheeks to marble. In Vietnam we had no weather like that. Here in Cleveland people call it spring. I walked half a block, then crossed the street and reached the vacant lot.

I stood tall and scouted. No one was sleeping on the old couch in the middle. I'd never entered the lot before, or wanted to. I did so now, picking my way between tires and trash bags. I nearly stepped on two rats gnawing and froze. Then I told myself that I must show my bravery. I continued farther and chose a spot far from the sidewalk and hidden from view by a rusty refrigerator. I had to keep my project safe.

I took out my spoon and began to dig. The snow had melted, but the ground was hard. After much work, I finished one hole, then a second, then a third. I thought about how my mother and sisters remembered my father, how they knew his face from every angle and held in their fingers the feel of his

"Kim" from *Seedfolks* by Paul Fleischman

hands. I had no such memories to cry over. I'd been born eight months after he'd died. Worse, he had no memories of me. When his spirit hovered over our altar, did it even know who I was?

I dug six holes. All his life in Vietnam my father had been a farmer. Here our apartment house had no yard. But in that vacant lot he would see me. He would watch my beans break ground and spread, and would notice with pleasure their pods growing plump. He would see my patience and my hard work. I would show him that I could raise plants, as he had. I would show him that I was his daughter.

My class had sprouted lima beans in paper cups the year before. I now placed a bean in each of the holes. I covered them up, pressing the soil down firmly with my fingertips. I opened my thermos and watered them all. And I vowed to myself that those beans would thrive.

●◆ How do Kim's thoughts help explain why she plants the seeds? Make some notes about Kim's thoughts and feelings before and while she plants the seeds.

Kim's thoughts and feelings before planting the beans:

Kim's thoughts and feelings while planting the beans:

Now imagine you are Kim. Write a journal entry in which you describe the many emotions you felt on that windy Sunday in April.

Understanding how a character thinks and feels can help you understand the character's actions.

Five
The Other Characters

You can uncover clues about a character by paying attention to the reactions of other characters. As you read these letters from Barbara Nichol's *Beethoven Lives Upstairs,* underline any clues you find about Christoph's and Uncle Karl's attitudes toward Beethoven.

Response notes

from ***Beethoven Lives Upstairs***
by Barbara Nichol

7 September 1822

Dear Uncle,

I hope you will remember me. It is Christoph, your nephew, who writes. As to the reasons, I will not keep you in suspense. I write, Uncle, because something terrible has happened. A madman has moved into our house.

Do you remember that when Father died, Mother decided to rent out his office upstairs? Well, she has done it, and Ludwig van Beethoven has moved in.

Every morning at dawn Mr. Beethoven begins to make his dreadful noise upstairs. Loud poundings and howlings come through the floor. They are like the sounds of an injured beast. All morning Mr. Beethoven carries on this way. After lunch he storms into the street. He comes home, sometimes long after the house is quiet for the night, tracking mud and stamping his way up the stairs above our heads.

Mother says I mustn't blame him. He's deaf and can't hear the noise he makes. But he wakes up the twins, and they start their crying. They cry all day.

Uncle, I must make this one request. I beg you to tell my mother to send Mr. Beethoven away.

Your nephew,
Christoph

69

Response notes

from ***Beethoven Lives Upstairs***
by Barbara Nichol

10 October 1822

My dear Christoph,

I arrived home last night to find your letter on the table in the hall. Do I remember you? Of course I do!

I should tell you that I received a letter from your mother as well. As you know, she is concerned about you and wants you to be happy. She assures me that Mr. Beethoven is peculiar perhaps, but certainly not mad.

Christoph, Mr. Beethoven will settle in soon, I'm sure. I know that life will be more peaceful before long.

Your uncle,
Karl

Response notes

from *Beethoven Lives Upstairs*
by Barbara Nichol

22 October 1822

Dear Uncle,

I hope you will forgive my troubling you, but I am sure that you will want to hear this news. Our family is now the laughingstock of Vienna.

I opened the door this morning to find a crowd in front of our house. They were looking up at Mr. Beethoven's window and laughing, so I looked up too. There was Mr. Beethoven, staring at a sheet of music. And Uncle, he had no clothes on at all! It was a dreadful sight!

You should see him setting out for the afternoon. He hums to himself. He growls out tunes. He waves his arms. His pockets bulge with papers and pencils. On the street the children run and call him names.

Mr. Beethoven is so famous that sometimes people stop outside our house, hoping they will see him. But if anyone asks, I say he has moved away.

Your nephew,
Christoph

70

These letters give two opinions of Beethoven—that of Christoph and his uncle. Based on what the characters think about Beethoven, what is your opinion of him?

●◆Remember that character you created in Lesson One? How would others react to him or her? Find out by putting the character in a brief scene with someone else. First create a second character. Use the chart to jot down some notes about the character.

MY CHARACTER

Character's name:	Relationship to first character:
What character looks like:	Sketch of character:

How character:

acts   thinks   talks

(Circle one and describe.)

●✦Now write your scene. Include descriptions of how the two characters you created look, speak, think, and act toward one another.

Paying attention to how characters react to each other can help you decide how you feel about the characters.

Author's Craft

Becoming an effective writer is like becoming an effective pianist or sculptor. It takes a lot of practice, hard work, and some special techniques.

Part of the pleasure of reading comes from seeing authors use their craft in masterful ways. In the lessons that follow, you will learn to recognize some of the techniques that authors practice and use as they craft their writing. These techniques include using:

- similes
- metaphors
- personification
- sensory language
- irony

One Surprising Comparisons

What's it like? That's the question that a simile answers. A **simile** is a comparison of two unlike things, often using the word *like* or *as*. Writers use similes to create unusual images and to help us see qualities or features in a new way.

Notice the similes in the following sentences.

> In the dark, the flashlight beam shone <u>like a yellow sword</u>.

> Raindrops <u>as big as quarters</u> splashed on the windowpane.

The first simile emphasizes the thinness and sharpness of the beam of light; the second describes the size of raindrops. When you read a simile, notice the images that it leaves in your mind.

Read the following poem twice. The first time through, read it for meaning. The second time, look for and underline similes.

Response notes

maggie and milly and molly and may
E. E. Cummings

maggie and milly and molly and may
went down to the beach(to play one day)

and maggie discovered a shell that sang
so sweetly she couldn't remember her troubles,and

milly befriended a stranded star
whose rays five languid fingers were;

and molly was chased by a horrible thing
which raced sideways while blowing bubbles:and

may came home with a smooth round stone
as small as a world and as large as alone.

For whatever we lose(like a you or a me)
it's always ourselves we find in the sea

●❖Describe or draw the images the similes leave in your mind.

●❖Try creating similes of your own. In the center of the web below, write one subject: a favorite (or least favorite) place, object, food, animal, or concept. Then write three or more similes to describe your subject. Try for original comparisons. For example, if your subject were your favorite pizza you might write "toppings bright and jumbled as a toy-store window" or "crust thick as a small mattress."

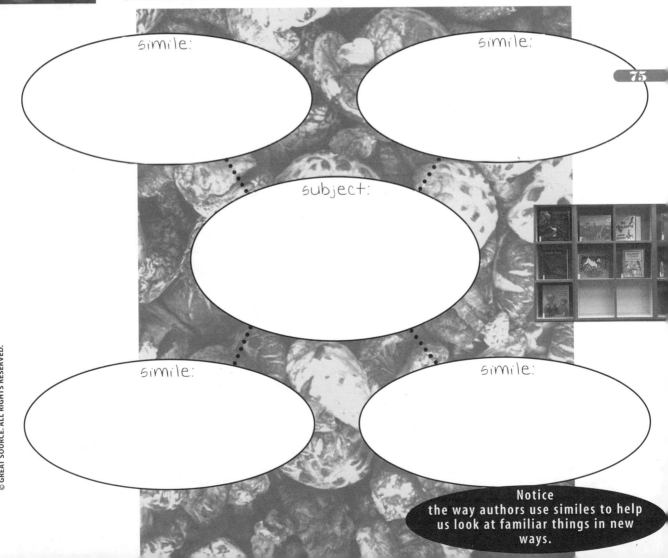

simile:

simile:

75

subject:

simile:

simile:

Notice
the way authors use similes to help
us look at familiar things in new
ways.

Two What It Is

A metaphor, like a simile, is a comparison of two unlike things. Metaphors, however, do not include the words *like* or *as*. Metaphors are compact. They let authors pack a great deal of meaning into only a few words, and they encourage readers to develop their own ideas about the things being compared.

Notice the comparisons in the metaphors below:

> *Love is a rose.*

> *Above our camp arched the sky, a blue bowl of light.*

The first metaphor compares love to a rose. The second compares the sky to a bowl. Each metaphor suggests ideas about the things being compared. For example, you might read "Love is a rose" and recall that a rose can be thorny as well as beautiful. What might this metaphor suggest about love?

In "Grape Sherbet," the poet recalls a special dessert that her father made at a family Memorial Day barbecue. Read the poem at least twice. Look for metaphors, and circle each one that you find. In your response notes, write the things that each metaphor compares. (See if you can spot a simile too.)

Response notes

grape sherbet = swirled snow

Grape Sherbet
Rita Dove

The day? Memorial.
After the grill
Dad appears with his masterpiece—
swirled snow, gelled light.
We cheer. The recipe's
a secret and he fights
a smile, his cap turned up
so the bib resembles a duck.

That morning we galloped
through the grassed-over mounds
and named each stone
for a lost milk tooth. Each dollop
of sherbet, later,
is a miracle,
like salt on a melon that makes it sweeter.

Response notes

Everyone agrees—it's wonderful!
It's just how we imagined lavender
would taste. The diabetic grandmother
stares from the porch,
a torch
of pure refusal.

We thought no one was lying
there under our feet,
we thought it
was a joke. I've been trying
to remember the taste,
but it doesn't exist.
Now I see why
you bothered,
father.

The speaker in the poem says, "Now I see why / you bothered, / father." Why do you think the father "bothers" to make his special dessert?

◖◆ Use the inside part of a Venn diagram to explore a metaphor. The model below shows how. Choose one metaphor that you found in "Grape Sherbet." On the lines under the Venn diagram, write the two things that the metaphor compares. In the overlapping part of the circles, write your own ideas about the two things' likenesses.

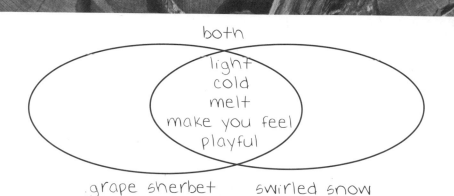

both

light
cold
melt
make you feel
playful

grape sherbet   swirled snow

Authors use metaphors to suggest new ways of seeing and understanding.

Three

Almost Human

Personification is a comparison in which a nonhuman thing is given human traits. By using personification, authors can make even ordinary objects come to life. Example:

Wind laughs around the corners of the buildings.

The wind can't really laugh, of course. But by using personification, the author makes the wind seem cheerful and playful. What characteristics about the wind might the following example of personification suggest?

Outside, the cold wind whined and complained.

In "The Fox and the Crow," it is not the wind but two animals that are given human traits. As you read, note ways in which these animals seem human.

The Fox and the Crow
Aesop

A crow was sitting on the branch of a tree with a stolen piece of cheese in her beak. A fox stood nearby and watched her, wishing to get hold of the cheese. The fox came closer, and standing beneath the tree, he began to compliment the crow on her size and beauty. He went so far as to say that she could be Queen of the Birds if only she had a voice. The crow, anxious to prove that she did possess a voice, began to caw vigorously. When she opened her beak, the cheese, of course, dropped to the ground. The fox pounced upon it and carried it off, remarking as he went away, "My good friend Crow, you have many good qualities; now try to get some common sense."

Response notes

79

●◆ What do you think of the fox?

●◆In the shapes below, write words that describe the human traits you noticed in the crow and the fox.

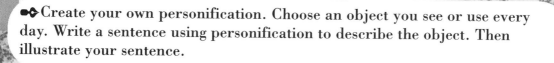

●◆Create your own personification. Choose an object you see or use every day. Write a sentence using personification to describe the object. Then illustrate your sentence.

80

Authors use personification to give nonhuman things human characteristics.

Four

See It, Hear It, Feel It . . .

Sensory language appeals to the five senses: sight, sound, taste, smell, and touch. Authors use sensory language to make their writing vivid. In some selections, an author may focus on only one or two senses. In other selections, an author may appeal to as many of the senses as possible.

As you read "Telephone Talk," notice which parts refer to things you can see, hear, taste, smell, and touch or feel (hardness, softness, warmth, or cold, for example). Mark each example of sensory language that you find.

Telephone Talk
X. J. Kennedy

Back flat on the carpet,
Cushion under my head,
Sock feet on the wallpaper,
Munching raisin bread,

Making easy whispers
Balance on high wire,
Trading jokes and laughing,
The two of us conspire,

Closer than when walking
Down the street together,
Closer than two sparrows
Hiding from wet weather.

How would my shrill whistle
Sound to you, I wonder?
Give a blow in your phone,
My phone makes it thunder.

Through the night, invisibly
Jumping over space,
Back and forth between us
All our secrets race.

Response notes

81

First, discuss the poem with a classmate. Describe the parts of the poem that are most vivid in your mind. Explore your questions, ideas, and feelings about the poem. Next, using your response notes, work together to fill in the chart below. Decide which senses the poem appeals to most and least.

phrases from poem	sight	sound	smell	taste	touch
munching raisin bread		✓	✓	✓	

82

●◆ Now work together to write one or more stanzas for "Telephone Talk."
Base your stanza on your own favorite ways to talk on the phone. Appeal to
the senses least represented on your chart.

Authors use
sensory language
to bring their
writing to life for
readers.

Five
It's a Twist

Some of the best literature involves surprising twists or turns of events. These twists and turns are sometimes examples of situational **irony**: an outcome that doesn't match what characters—or readers—might reasonably expect. Authors often use irony to create humor. At the same time, an ironic twist can offer a thought-provoking insight about human beings or about life.

As you read "Almost Perfect," put stars by the parts that you like best. Do any of these parts involve unexpected outcomes?

Response notes

Almost Perfect
Shel Silverstein

"Almost perfect . . . but not quite."
Those were the words of Mary Hume
At her seventh birthday party,
Looking 'round the ribboned room.
"This tablecloth is *pink*, not *white*—
Almost perfect . . . but not quite."

"Almost perfect . . . but not quite."
Those were the words of grown-up Mary
Talking about her handsome beau,
The one she wasn't gonna marry.
"Squeezes me a bit too tight—
Almost perfect . . . but not quite."

"Almost perfect . . . but not quite."
Those were the words of ol' Miss Hume
Teaching in the seventh grade,
Grading papers in the gloom,
Late at night up in her room.
"They never cross their t's just right—
Almost perfect . . . but not quite."

Ninety-eight the day she died
Complainin' 'bout the spotless floor.
People shook their heads and sighed,
"Guess that she'll like heaven more."
Up went her soul on feathered wings,
Out the door, up out of sight.
Another voice from heaven came—
"Almost perfect . . . but not quite."

●◆ What do you think of Miss Mary Hume? Have you ever known anyone like her?

●◆ Given what you know about Miss Mary Hume, what would you have *expected* to happen at the end of this poem?

●◆ Read the poem again. Explain what happens at the end of the poem and what makes this ending ironic.

Irony is one technique authors use to add humor and depth to their writing.

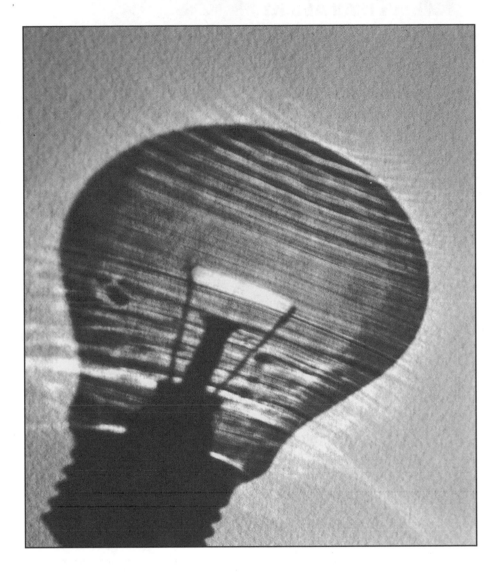

The Art of Argument

Writing a strong argument is like fishing. You could just drop a line with a hook tied to it in a lake and hope that a fish will bite. But if you really wanted to catch a fish, you would probably add a juicy worm or maybe even a fancy lure. Writers of arguments try to "hook" their readers too. They want their readers to share their viewpoint on a topic.

Just as some kinds of bait are better at catching fish, some arguments are better at convincing readers to share an author's viewpoint. When you understand writers' strategies for making arguments, you'll be able to decide whether an argument you read is a convincing one.

One

What's It All About?

The point of an argument is called the **main idea**. It's the message that the author is trying to send you. Often the main idea will explain the writer's **opinion**.

In "A Uniformly Good Idea," the writer presents his opinion on a particular subject—school uniforms. As you read the article, think to yourself, "What does the writer think about school uniforms? What is the writer's opinion?" Jot down your ideas in the response notes.

"A Uniformly Good Idea" by Steve Forbes

Schools across the country should follow the example of Long Beach, Calif., which is requiring public-school students to wear uniforms.

The case for uniforms is overwhelming. They are democratic: Regardless of background, no youngster stands out because of his or her clothes. Uniforms help sharpen kids' focus on the task at hand—schoolwork. Too many students spend an inordinate amount of time worrying about what they should wear. Uniforms underscore that the purpose of school is learning, not making fashion statements. In well-run schools, uniforms will help develop an esprit de corps that will improve youngsters' educational performances.

Such a rigid dress code will aid in reducing violence. Kids are less likely to be accosted and robbed and perhaps even shot for expensive apparel or jewelry. Uniforms subtly decrease the influence of gangs whose members have set themselves apart by their distinctive garments. Uniforms also help identify outsiders, who are usually at school to stir up trouble.

Uniforms reinforce a valuable principle: Judge people not by their appearances but by their characters.

Perverse-minded critics carp that such dress codes will lessen youngsters' individuality. Hogwash. Kids will learn that they can distinguish themselves in more substantive ways, such as through performance in academics or sports or other extracurricular activities, rather than in the superficial way of slapping on what they think at the moment is a smart set of clothes.

What is the main idea of this article? Find and underline the sentences that best state the main idea.

●◆ What is Forbes's viewpoint on school uniforms? Do you share Forbes's opinion? Write a letter to the editor of your local newspaper explaining your opinion on school uniforms.

89

Finding the main idea of an argument helps you understand the writer's viewpoint.

Two With Good Reason

Imagine you want your parents to buy you a new bike. If you just say, "I want a bike," they may not be convinced. But if you give them reasons why ("I'll get more exercise, and you won't have to drive me everywhere"), they might "buy" your argument. (And they also might buy you the bike!)

Writers of convincing arguments support their viewpoints with reasons and details. Look back to Steve Forbes's article about school uniforms. What supporting **details** does he give to back up his **opinion**? Reread the article, putting stars in the margin near the supporting details.

●◆ Use a web to show how details support the main idea of Forbes's article. Write the main idea of this article in the circle. (The circle will become the middle of the web.) From the circle, draw an "arm" for each supporting detail.

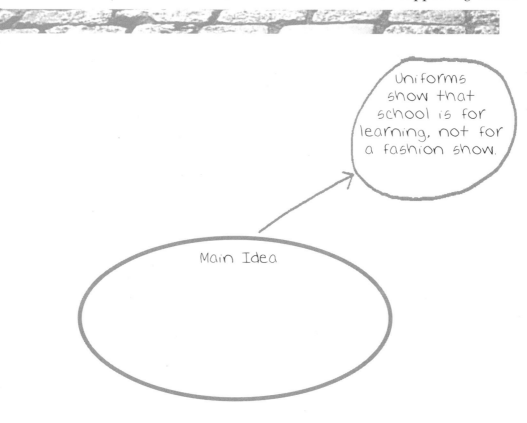

Uniforms show that school is for learning, not for a fashion show.

Main Idea

●◆Now try using details to support an argument of your own. Choose a topic on which you and your parents have different opinions (for example, allowance or phone privileges). Write your parents a note, using supporting details to convince them to share your viewpoint. Before you begin, create a main idea/details web to help you organize your argument.

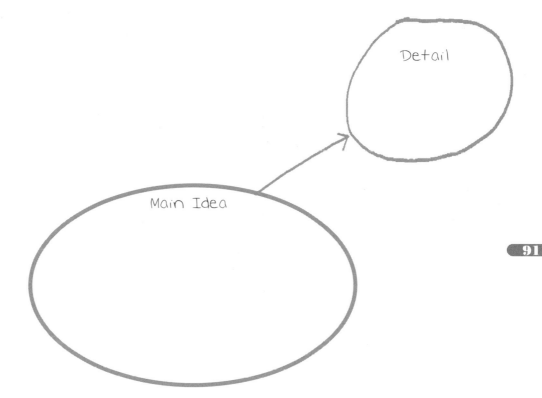

Detail

Main Idea

●➤ Write a note to your parents in the space below. Begin by clearly stating your main idea. Then build your argument using supporting details.

Writers
use details and reasons
to support the main idea
of an argument.

Three

Seeing the Other Side

There are at least two sides to every argument. (After all, it wouldn't be much of an argument if nobody disagreed with you.) Writers of convincing arguments know that the best way to counter opposing **viewpoints** is to tackle them head-on by explaining how and why the opposing arguments are wrong.

As you read this excerpt from "Robots Will Never Replace Humans," ask yourself: "What is the writer's viewpoint on the topic?" "How does she handle opposing viewpoints?" Circle words or phrases that help you answer these questions.

from **"Robots Will Never Replace Humans"** by Rosa Velasquez

Response notes

In movies and science fiction novels, we've seen many kinds of talking robots. They are always smart and well-behaved, and walk like people. That creature, however, simply doesn't exist in the real world. The popular image of robots has misled people from the start. When industrial robots were invented, we expected them to look and think like us, but, in fact, they didn't. Nor is it likely they ever will. Engineers believe there's little reason to try to build a "mechanical human being." Even a baby less than two years old can do three things no robot can: recognize a face, understand a human language, and walk on two legs. If they can't do everything a person can, then robots will never replace humans.

Robots do have their place, however. They can perform certain tasks, such as building car bodies in factories and stacking boxes for shipping. These kinds of jobs they do very well. And it is the dangerous and boring tasks that robots do best—those jobs that no person enjoys. During the early 1960s, the first industrial robots lifted a piece of metal from a conveyer belt, drilled a hole in it, and returned it to the conveyor belt. Before, human workers would perform the same task hour after hour, sometimes feeling like little more than robots themselves.

In the article, Rosa Velasquez includes details to support both her viewpoint and the opposing one. Does including the opposing viewpoint strengthen or weaken Velasquez's argument? Explain.

....

....

....

....

....

93

👉 In the chart below, write Velasquez's viewpoint at the top of the left column. Write the opposing viewpoint at the top of the right column. Under each heading, write the details from the article that support each viewpoint.

Velasquez's Viewpoint:	Opposing Viewpoint:
Details:	Details:

👉 Review the note you wrote to your parents in Lesson Two. What arguments could they make to support their "side"? Write a paragraph to put in your letter that describes (and refutes!) their argument.

Writers include (and refute) opposing viewpoints to strengthen their own.

Four
That's a Fact!

A fact is something that can be proven to be true or false. It is a fact, for example, that water freezes at zero degrees centigrade. An **opinion** is something that someone believes is true, but cannot be proven true or false. (For instance, "Michael Jordan is the greatest basketball player who ever lived.") Arguments are opinions, but writers of convincing arguments know that facts can make their opinions more convincing.

Look back at "Robots Will Never Replace Humans." Use a yellow marker to highlight opinions in the article. Use a green marker to highlight facts. Then use arrows to connect each fact with the opinion it supports. (Tip: More than one fact will support each opinion.)

●◆Support an opinion of your own. Imagine that you are on a committee whose job is to give an award for "The Best _____." In a small group, fill in the blank (with something like *television show*, *football team*, or *fast-food place*). Then make a list of facts to support your opinion.

THE BEST _____

Looking for facts will help you decide if an argument is a convincing one.

Five
Good Point?

When you evaluate an argument, you decide whether the argument is convincing. You might not always agree with what the writer has to say (you may not *want* to wear a uniform to school), but the writer may still make a good argument in favor of his or her **viewpoint**.

As you read this excerpt, think about the author's viewpoint. How does he support it? Circle or underline any strategies he uses, such as using supporting details and **facts**, and refuting opposing arguments.

← Response notes

from *Green Planet Rescue* by Robert R. Halpern

"Endangered" sounds like something scary, and it is. "Danger" is right there in the middle of it. But when the subject is endangered plants, it's hard to see what all the fuss is about. Plants just grow, don't they? Weeds sprout in every open space, so what's the problem? There are always plenty of green things out there—everywhere we look. Why is any one plant species all that important?

Plants are not great as pets, but they are our companions on this planet. They are important in our lives and in the lives of every other animal. They produce the basic resources for life on Earth. There may be 380,000 or more different species of plants and we know little about many of them. Some species live in such special and small habitats that we haven't even found them yet. Can we afford to find out what life without a particular species would be like?

An endangered species is one with a small population whose survival is threatened. Human populations are growing. New roads, buildings, dams, farms, and grazing areas are spreading over the landscape so that little real wilderness is left anywhere. An endangered species will disappear if these conditions continue. An endangered species needs help. Today 20,000 to 25,000 of the plant species on Earth are endangered, vulnerable, or rare. We may be losing something important without even knowing much about it.

●◆Imagine that you are a teacher, and one of your students turned in this article for an assignment on endangered species. On the following form, give it a letter grade based on how well the student supports his or her argument. Remember, you are deciding how effective the argument is, not whether or not you agree with the writer's viewpoint.

DOES THE AUTHOR:

❏ CLEARLY STATE HIS OR HER MAIN IDEA

❏ PROVIDE DETAILS TO SUPPORT THE MAIN IDEA

❏ INCLUDE FACTS TO BACK UP HIS OR HER OPINIONS

❏ REFUTE OPPOSING ARGUMENTS

GRADE ASSIGNED FOR THIS ARTICLE IS: ....

REASONS FOR THIS GRADE: ....

....

....

....

....

....

....

....

....

....

....

....

....

....

97

●◆ Put the strategies you've learned for writing a convincing argument to work. In a small group, decide on a local issue you'd like to comment on. You might, for example, want to change a ban on skateboarding in parking lots or encourage others to recycle. Write a proposal to submit to your mayor. Be sure it includes a clear opinion and facts to support it. You should also consider how you'll deal with opposing viewpoints.

To evaluate an argument, look for details and facts that support the opinion.

Focus on the Writer: Lois Lowry

It was simply what I always wanted to do, from childhood: what I did best, loved best. I have never wanted to do anything but write. To shape, to create and compose, to shed light, to perceive and pass on.

—*Lois Lowry*

Lois Lowry's love of writing is evident in the more than twenty novels she has written, two of them Newbery Medal winners. In nearly all of her books, Lowry draws upon her own experiences and the experiences of people she knows. Some of Lowry's books depict settings in which she has lived, others have characters based on people she has known, and still others depict events from her own life. As you read works by Lois Lowry, think about how she has "put herself" into her writing.

Writing from Experience

Lowry often draws on the relationships within her own family when she creates characters for her books. Growing up, Lowry had two siblings, an older sister, who died of cancer at a young age, and a younger brother. In her writing, Lowry focuses on the roles that people play in the lives of others. In fact, she has said that all of her books deal with the same basic theme: the importance of human connections.

In *A Summer to Die*, Lowry explores the intense sibling rivalry between two sisters. Thirteen-year-old Meg is jealous of her pretty and popular older sister, Molly. In this excerpt, Molly (who has spent time in the hospital due to a mysterious illness) desperately wants to keep her new symptoms a secret. As you read, pay attention to how Meg (the narrator) and Molly act toward each other. Put an "X" in the response notes near incidents and phrases that remind you of real siblings.

response notes

from *A Summer to Die* by Lois Lowry

She was grouchy and mad, too. I'm not sure why. I think mostly it was because school had just ended, before she'd even had a chance to go back. Tierney McGoldrick hardly ever calls her anymore. She doesn't know it, but toward the end of school he started dating a red-haired senior girl. At least I was smart enough not to tell Molly *that.*

But there she was, lying on her bed, grumbling about how awful she looks. I am so sick of hearing Molly talk about how she looks. Her face is too fat. Her hair is too thin. To hear her talk, you'd think she was really a mess, when the truth is that she's still a billion times prettier than I am, which is why I'm sick of listening to her.

I told her to shut up.

She told me to drop dead, and before I dropped dead, to pick up my sneakers from her side of the room.

I told her to pick them up herself.

She started to get up, I think to pick up my sneakers and throw them at me, and when she swung her legs over the side of the bed, I suddenly saw what they looked like.

"Molly!" I said, forgetting about the sneakers. "What's wrong with your *legs?*"

"What do you *mean*, what's wrong with my legs?" No one had ever criticized Molly's legs before; in fact, even I have to admit that Molly's got nice legs. She held up her nightgown and looked down.

Both of her legs were covered with dark red spots. It looked like a lot of mosquito bites, except that they weren't swollen.

from *A Summer to Die* by Lois Lowry

"Does it hurt?"

"No," she said slowly, looking puzzled. "What could it be? It wasn't there yesterday; I know it wasn't."

"Well, it's there now, and it sure looks weird."

She pulled her nightgown down to cover her legs. Then she got into bed and pulled the covers up around her. "Don't tell anyone," she said.

"I will, too. I'm telling Mom." I started out of the room.

"Don't you *dare*," Molly ordered.

I'll be darned if I'll take orders from Molly. Anyway, I really thought my parents ought to know. I went downstairs and told Mom that there was something wrong with Molly's legs; she jumped up with a frightened look and went upstairs. I stayed out of it after that, but I listened.

I heard Mom and Molly arguing. I heard my mother get my father from the study. Then more arguing with Molly. I heard my mother go to the upstairs phone, make a call, and go back to Molly.

Then Molly crying. Yelling. I had never in my life heard Molly like that before. She was screaming, "No! I won't! I won't!"

Things quieted down after a few minutes, and then my father came down. His face was very drawn, very tired. "We have to take Molly back to the hospital," he told me abruptly, and without waiting for me to answer, he went out to start the car.

Mom came downstairs with Molly. She was in her bathrobe and slippers, and she was sobbing. When they were by the front door, Molly saw me standing all alone in the living room. She turned to me, still crying, and said, "I hate you! I hate you!"

"Molly," I whispered, "please don't."

What kind of relationship do Meg and Molly have? Who do you feel sympathy for, Meg, Molly—or both? Note which parts of the text help shape your opinion.

●◆Look back at your response notes. How are Molly and Meg like real sisters that you know—or like you and your brother or sister? Think of a pair of siblings, either yourself and a sibling or siblings you have heard or read about. Use the Venn diagram to compare and contrast them to Molly and Meg.

Meg and Molly

Both

Other siblings

Writers draw on experiences and relationships in their own lives to create realistic characters and situations in their stories.

Two
Tackling Tough Issues

In some of her books Lowry tackles tough issues, such as the difficulties of dealing with mental illness and divorce and coping with death. Lowry does not write about these issues to make people sad. She writes about them to give people hope and make them realize that they are strong enough to face their problems—with the help of others.

In *A Summer to Die*, Meg eventually realizes that her sister Molly is going to die. Because she faced the death of her own sister when she was young, Lowry was able to write with a lot of personal understanding. In the following excerpt, Meg and her father have a conversation about what is happening to Molly. As you read the dialogue, underline passages that you think are important, and reflect on their meaning in the response notes.

Response notes

from **A Summer to Die** by Lois Lowry

Dad drove me to Portland, and on the way he tried to tell me what it would be like at the hospital. "You have to keep reminding yourself," he said, "that it's still Molly. That's the hard thing, for me. Every time I go in her room, it takes me by surprise, seeing all that machinery. It seems to separate you from her. You have to look past it, and see that it's still Molly. Do you understand?"

I shook my head. "No," I said.

Dad sighed. "Well, I'm not sure I do either. But listen, Meg— when you think of Molly, how do you think of her?"

I was quiet for a minute, thinking. "I guess mostly I think of how she used to laugh. And then I think of how, even after she got sick, she used to run out in the field on sunny mornings, looking for new flowers. I used to watch her, sometimes, from the window."

"That's what I mean. That's the way I think of Molly, too. But when you get to the hospital, you'll see that everything is different for Molly now. It will make you feel strange, because you're outside of it; you're not part of it.

"She'll be very sleepy. That's because of the drugs they're giving her, so that she'll feel comfortable. And she can't talk to you, because there's a tube in her throat to help her breathe.

"She'll look like a stranger to you, at first. And it'll be scary. But she can hear you, Meg. Talk to her. And you'll realize that underneath all that stuff, the tubes and needles and medicines, our Molly is still there. You have to remember that. It makes it easier.

"And, Meg?" He was driving very carefully, following the white line in the center of the curving road.

from *A Summer to Die* by Lois Lowry

"What?"

"One more thing. Remember, too, that Molly's not in any pain, and she's not scared. It's only you and I and Mom, now, who are hurting and frightened.

"This is a hard thing to explain, Meg, but Molly is handling this thing very well by herself. She needs us, for our love, but she doesn't need us for anything else now." He swallowed hard and said, "Dying is a very solitary thing. The only thing we can do is be there when she wants us there."

●◆Look back at your response notes. What important lesson or message is Meg's father trying to convey? Would you find his words comforting if you were Meg? Why or why not?

●◆Like Lowry, you could write about experiences that have helped you learn more about life and relationships. In the "Experience Bank" below, jot down some situations or problems that you have faced—they don't all have to be sad or serious. Then circle the ones that you would most like to write about.

Writers tackle tough issues to show that there are lessons that can be learned from difficult situations.

Three

Painting a Picture

Did you know that in addition to being a writer, Lois Lowry is also a photographer? Lois Lowry has compared the job of a writer to the job of a photographer: she notes that a writer has to choose the best "lens" and setting for his or her work, deciding which things to focus on and which things to blur.

Lowry uses **details** to give her work focus and to paint vivid pictures in the minds of readers. The **setting** of Lowry's novel *Autumn Street* is the same town in which Lowry lived during World War II. Lowry's father was fighting in the war, so she, her mother, and her sister lived with her grandparents in central Pennsylvania. As you read, underline details of the setting that are clear, or "in focus." Circle the details that are "blurry" in the narrator's description.

← Response notes

106

from *Autumn Street* by Lois Lowry

It was a long time ago.

Though it seems, sometimes, that most things that matter happened a long time ago, that is not really true. What is true is this: by the time you realize how much something mattered, time has passed; by the time it stops hurting enough that you can tell about it, first to yourself, and finally to someone else, more time has passed; then, when you sit down to begin the telling, you have to begin this way:

It was a long time ago.

If, instead of a pencil, I held a brush in my hand, I would paint the scene: the scene of Autumn Street. Perspective wouldn't matter; it would be distorted and askew, as it was through my own eyes when I was six, and Grandfather's house would loom huge, out of proportion, awesome and austere, with the clipped lawn as smooth and green as patchwork pockets on a velvet skirt. The rough pink brick of the sidewalk, bordered by elms, would wind the length of the street, past the Hoffmans' house, past the bright forsythia bushes that grew around the great-aunts' front porch, past the homes of strangers and friends and forgotten people, finally disappearing where the woods began.

Even today, with a brush, I would blur the woods. I would blur them with a murky mixture of brown and green and black, the hueless shade that I know from my dreams to be the color of pain.

But the sky above Autumn Street would be resplendent blue. In the sky, the painted ghosts would flutter, hovering like Chagall angels, benevolently smiling down on the strip of Pennsylvania where they had peopled a year of my life. Grandfather would be there in the sky, sailing past, holding his

© GREAT SOURCE. ALL RIGHTS RESERVED.

from *Autumn Street* by Lois Lowry

cane, wearing his most elegant suit, his tie in place and his
hair impeccably brushed. Grandmother wouldn't sail; she would
hover primly in the most tasteful and protected corner of the
heaven, buttoned to her chin and holding her ankles neatly
crossed. The great-aunts would soar grandly by, holding hands
and tittering, a trio of good manners and barely contained
laughter, wearing gauzy dresses that billowed.

◗◆Look back at the details you circled and underlined. What feelings do you
think cause the narrator to "blur" some aspects of the setting?

◗◆What did you picture in your mind as you read about Autumn Street?
Put the picture in your mind on paper—draw a sketch of Autumn Street as
it looks through the eyes of the narrator.

◆◇ Think of a place that has been important in your life. What details would you include if you were describing it? Make a web to gather your thoughts. Write the name of the place in the middle of the web. Draw arms to list details about the place. Choose details that convey your overall feeling about the place.

Detail

Place

Detail

Focus on details as you read to create mental pictures of the setting and learn about characters.

Four Making History Come Alive

In addition to using her own experiences and settings from her own life in her stories, Lois Lowry has also used events in history to create a story. When writers blend actual historical **facts** with imaginary **details**, they are writing **historical fiction**.

Lois Lowry's book *Number the Stars*, which won the Newbery Medal, tells the story of a family in Denmark who helped their Jewish friends escape to Sweden during World War II to avoid relocation by the Nazis. In the Afterword to the book, Lowry explains how she blends fact with fictional details to tell a powerful and moving story:

FROM THE AFTERWORD TO *NUMBER THE STARS* BY LOIS LOWRY

How much of Annemarie's story is true? I know I will be asked that. Let me try to tell you, here, where fact ends and fiction begins.

Annemarie Johansen is a child of my imagination, though she grew there from the stories told to me by my friend Annelise Platt, to whom this book is dedicated, who was herself a child in Copenhagen during the long years of the German occupation.

I had always been fascinated and moved by Annelise's descriptions not only of the personal deprivation that her family and their neighbors suffered during those years, and the sacrifices they made, but even more by the greater picture she drew for me of the courage and integrity of the Danish people under the leadership of the king they loved so much, Christian X.

So I created little Annemarie and her family, set them down in a Copenhagen apartment on a street where I have walked myself, and imagined their life there against the real events of 1943.

In the following passage from *Number the Stars*, Lowry describes a harrowing night that Annemarie's family spends with their friend, Ellen Rosen. As you read, look for details that are historical facts and details that Lowry has made up. Write "fact" and "fiction" in the response notes near the appropriate parts.

from ***Number the Stars*** by Lois Lowry

Response notes

Though Mrs. Rosen had sent her chicken to the Johansens, and Mama made a lovely dinner large enough for second helpings all around, it was not an evening of laughter and talk. Ellen was silent at dinner. She looked frightened. Mama and Papa tried to speak of cheerful things, but it was clear that they were worried, and it made Annemarie worry, too. Only

Kirsti was unaware of the quiet tension in the room. Swinging her feet in their newly blackened and shiny shoes, she chattered and giggled during dinner.

"Early bedtime tonight, little one," Mama announced after the dishes were washed. "We need extra time for the long story I promised, about the king and queen." She disappeared with Kirsti into the bedroom.

"What's happening?" Annemarie asked when she and Ellen were alone with Papa in the living room. "Something's wrong. What is it?"

Papa's face was troubled. "I wish that I could protect you children from this knowledge," he said quietly. "Ellen, you already know. Now we must tell Annemarie."

He turned to her and stroked her hair with his gentle hand. "This morning, at the synagogue, the rabbi told his congregation that the Nazis have taken the synagogue lists of all the Jews. Where they live, what their names are. Of course the Rosens were on that list, along with many others."

"Why? Why did they want those names?"

"They plan to arrest all the Danish Jews. They plan to take them away. And we have been told that they may come tonight."

"I don't understand! Take them where?"

Her father shook his head. "We don't know where, and we don't really know why. They call it 'relocation.' We don't even know what that means. We only know that it is wrong, and it is dangerous, and we must help."

Annemarie was stunned. She looked at Ellen and saw that her best friend was crying silently.

"Where are Ellen's parents? We must help them, too!"

"We couldn't take all three of them. If the Germans came to search our apartment, it would be clear that the Rosens were here. One person we can hide. Not three. So Peter has helped Ellen's parents to go elsewhere. We don't know where. Ellen doesn't know either. But they are safe."

Ellen sobbed aloud, and put her face in her hands. Papa put his arm around her. "They are safe, Ellen. I promise you that. You will see them again quite soon. Can you try hard to believe my promise?"

Ellen hesitated, nodded, and wiped her eyes with her hand.

"But, Papa," Annemarie said, looking around the small apartment, with its few pieces of furniture: the fat stuffed sofa, the table and chairs, the small bookcase against the wall. "You said that we would hide her. How can we do that? Where can she hide?"

Papa smiled. "That part is easy. It will be as your mama said: you two will sleep together in your bed, and you may

from *Number the Stars* by Lois Lowry

giggle and talk and tell secrets to each other. And if anyone comes—"

Ellen interrupted him. "Who might come? Will it be soldiers? Like the ones on the corners?" Annemarie remembered how terrified Ellen had looked the day when the soldier had questioned them on the corner.

"I really don't think anyone will. But it never hurts to be prepared. If anyone should come, even soldiers, you two will be sisters. You are together so much, it will be easy for you to pretend that you are sisters."

He rose and walked to the window. He pulled the lace curtain aside and looked down into the street. Outside, it was beginning to grow dark. Soon they would have to draw the black curtains that all Danes had on their windows; the entire city had to be completely darkened at night. In a nearby tree, a bird was singing; otherwise it was quiet. It was the last night of September.

Look back at your response notes. Were you able to figure out how Lois Lowry blended historical facts with fictional details? Explain.

●→Instead of giving facts and figures about the Germans and their plans to relocate the Jewish people in Denmark, Lowry created believable characters to show you what it would have been like to have lived during the German occupation. How did reading the story make you feel? Did you connect with any of the characters? If so, which ones and why? Write a letter to Lois Lowry. Let her know how reading this excerpt made you feel.

112

Writers of historical fiction blend events that happened in history with fictional details to make history come "alive."

Five

Where Do Stories Come From?

When Lois Lowry won the Newbery Award for *Number the Stars,* she gave a speech to explain how she got her ideas for the story. Her friend Annelise gave Lowry the basic framework and the inspiration to write the story, but the book is full of details of day-to-day life that make the experiences of the characters seem so real. Where did Lowry get these day-to-day details? She did some research, interviewed people, and visited Denmark.

As you read Lowry's Newbery acceptance speech, note the methods and sources she used to track down realistic details to add to her story. In the response notes, jot down some of her methods.

from Lois Lowry's Newbery acceptance speech

She [Annelise] introduced me to a woman in Copenhagen named Kirsten Krogh, an older woman who was a young bride at the time of the German occupation. It was Kirsten Krogh—who with her husband had been involved in the Resistance movement—who told me what novel a young mother would have read, and loved, during those years. It surprised me. *Gone with the Wind?* An American novel about a feisty Southerner named Scarlett who pushed and shoved her way around Atlanta as it burned?

But I shouldn't have been surprised, because it connected with something else that Kirsten Krogh told me. When I asked her what was the worst single thing she remembered from those years, she thought about her answer for a long time. Then she said: "the powerlessness."

Of *course* they loved Scarlett O'Hara. I put *Gone with the Wind* in the book, too.

And it was Kirsten Krogh who told me what flowers would be in bloom along the Danish coast in autumn, and, in telling me, reminded me that flowers continue to bloom in terrible times, and that children still play with kittens.

I put in the flowers, and a kitten.

In Denmark I collected countless details to add to those that Annelise and Kirsten told me of their own lives during the war years. In Copenhagen I saw a pair of shoes made from fish skin. It was true, of course, that during the occupation the Danes couldn't import anything, so there was no leather for shoes. And surely it was a marvel of ingenuity that they figured out how to make shoes from the skin of fish.

But when I saw the shoes, I didn't think about the economic consequences of war. I couldn't even marvel at the craftsmanship or the cleverness, because I was living, by then, completely in

Response notes

113

the consciousness of a little girl: a little girl who wouldn't know—or care—about imports or economics. All I could think was what that child would think, on being given such a pair of shoes: Oh, they're so *ugly*.

And I put the ugly shoes, and the child's reaction, into the book.

When I asked Annelise to describe, through the eyes of her own childhood, the German soldiers themselves, she said: "I remember the high shiny boots...."

I certainly did use—and use and use—those high shiny boots. Annelise had mentioned them first; and then, when I pored over the old photographs, I saw them myself, again and again.

●◆Look back at your notes. What did Lowry do to prepare for writing *Number the Stars*? Write Lowry's "recipe" for creating historical fiction—list her "ingredients," how much of each she used, and how she blended them together to create a story.

114

Recipe for _____

Ingredients: Amounts:

_____

_____

_____

_____

_____

Directions for blending: _____

_____

_____

_____

Challenging Reading

Imagine that you are standing at the bottom of a mountain and you want to climb up. Would you just start climbing and hope for the best? What if you ran into slippery rocks? a steep incline? a sudden snowstorm? Climbing a mountain is full of challenges. But with the right tools and some preparation, it can be done.

Just like climbing a mountain, reading certain types of writing can be a challenge. You may come across difficult words or new ideas.

And just as a mountain climber has certain tools or strategies to help him or her reach the top, you can use strategies both before and during reading that will help you understand—and enjoy— challenging reading material.

One Using What You Already Know

Before tackling a mountain, climbers use what they already know to prepare: Is this mountain like other mountains they have climbed? What techniques would work best? What challenges might they expect to encounter?

Just as the climber uses what he or she already knows, you can use what you already know when you read. You can probably look at a selection and tell whether it's fiction or nonfiction. And, after reading the title and first paragraph or two, you may realize that you already know something about the topic.

Read the title and first paragraph of this piece of nonfiction. Think about what you already know about the topic.

response notes

from *And Then There Was One* by Margery Facklam

Dinosaurs dominated the earth for 160 million years—far longer than we humans have. Then, 65 million years ago, they disappeared. Why?

➥ A K-W-L Chart is one way to organize your thoughts before, during, and after your reading. What do you already know about dinosaurs? In the "K" section, write down everything that comes to your mind about these creatures. (Leave the other two columns blank for now.)

K-W-L CHART: DINOSAURS

K What I Know	**W** What I Want to Find Out	**L** What I Have Learned

●◆ Have fun with the facts you've written down in the "K" column of the K-W-L Chart. Use what you know about dinosaurs to create a cartoon strip about them.

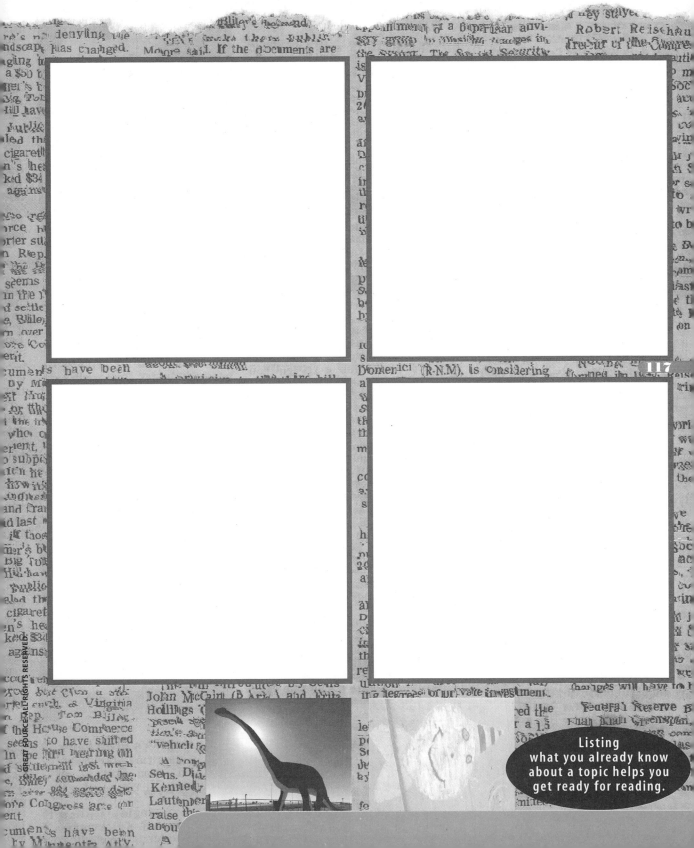

Listing
what you already know
about a topic helps you
get ready for reading.

Two Asking Questions

Look in the "K" column at the things you already know about dinosaurs. What else would you like to know? What questions do you think the article will answer? Before you read, write down any questions that you have. Then return to your K–W–L Chart on page 116 and put your questions under "W"—What I Want to Find Out. Here is the beginning of one reader's K-W-L chart:

K What I Know	**W** What I Want to Find Out	**L** What I Have Learned
Dinosaurs had small brains.	Did dinosaurs die because they weren't smart?	

The "W" column of your K-W-L Chart helps focus your reading. Pretend you are on a scavenger hunt—look for the answers to the questions as you read. Circle anything you find in the article that answers your questions. If more questions come up as you read, add them to the "W" column on the chart.

from ***And Then There Was One*** by Margery Facklam

Response notes

No one knows how bright or stupid dinosaurs may have been. After all, how do you judge an animal's intelligence? The skulls of some dinosaurs show they had small brains. Others, such as the tyrannosaurs, had big brains, but that didn't seem to matter. None of them survived.

It's likely that small mammals ate dinosaur eggs, but there were just too many dinosaurs of all shapes and sizes for mammals to have eaten enough eggs to kill them all. We know of at least one kind of dinosaur, *Maiasaura* (my-uh-SORE-uh), the "good mother lizard," that traveled in herds of 10,000 or more. The females laid their eggs in colonies of carefully spaced nests, similar to present-day nesting sites of penguins in Antarctica. After the eggs hatched, the female maiasaurs guarded and fed their young until they were big enough to follow the herd. Surely these big dinosaurs could have tromped on or scared away small mammals searching for their eggs. Yet, the maiasaurs died out, too.

John Horner, the scientist who discovered the "good mother lizard," also found one enormous deposit of bones where a

© GREAT SOURCE. ALL RIGHTS RESERVED.

from *And Then There Was One* by Margery Facklam

Response notes

huge herd of maiasaurs had been killed by gas and dust from erupting volcanoes. But hundreds of different kinds of dinosaurs were spread so far and wide that it's not likely that a few volcanic eruptions or earthquakes could have destroyed them all.

Dinosaurs didn't disappear in a weekend. Long before the final extinction, there were many dramatic events in nature, such as volcanoes and earthquakes, that wiped out some species. Disease epidemics also proved to be disastrous for many of the dinosaurs that moved out of old territories in search of more plentiful food and new breeding grounds.

As ancient continents began to shift and break apart, new continents were formed. Land bridges across shallow seas appeared where none had been before. Huge herds of Asian dinosaurs paraded across these land bridges in great migrations. That's when they may have met the germs and bacteria that Dr. Robert Baker calls the "death-dealing tourists."

When Europeans came to the Americas, they brought with them some "death-dealing tourists" such as chicken pox, measles, and other diseases the Native Americans had never had. Many native people died from these diseases because they weren't immune to them: they had no natural protection. It's likely that dinosaurs had no natural protection from the germs they picked up as they moved into new territories. Many dinosaurs could have died, and others, weakened by disease, probably didn't breed or lay eggs or have young.

Disease, changing food supplies, and growing competition from other animals killed off many species of dinosaurs, but the final blow to the Age of Reptiles may have come from space. Some scientists think that an asteroid or huge meteorite may have crashed into the earth. It would have exploded with a force thousands of times more powerful than that of all the nuclear weapons on earth. Poisonous gases would have swirled around the world in windstorms traveling thousands of miles an hour. The dust and fires would have blackened the skies for months or years. Without sunlight, plants would have died first, and the plant eaters soon after.

119

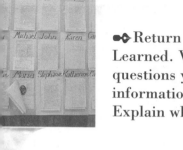

●◆Return to the K-W-L Chart and fill in the "L" column—What I Have Learned. What you write in the "L" column should include answers to the questions you wrote in the "W" column. Were you surprised by any of the information in the article? Were you able to answer all of your questions? Explain whether the K-W-L Chart helped you as you read.

●◆Write down 3–4 additional questions you have about dinosaurs in the space below. Then exchange *Daybook*s with a partner and try to answer each other's questions.

120

Asking questions before and while you are reading gives you a purpose for reading.

Adjusting Your Speed

Think back to the mountain climbers. When they get to a really steep part of the mountain, they probably slow down. When they are on a gentle slope, they can probably hike faster. And, if they lose their footing and slip, they need to find a different and better way to cover the same ground.

When you read a challenging piece of writing, you can use the same kinds of strategies that a mountain climber uses. You can:

- Change the pace of your reading by reading more quickly when the material is easy and by reading more slowly when you come across difficult words or concepts.

- Read something again when you have trouble understanding it the first time.

- Stop while you are reading to ask yourself a question and read on to find the answer. (You probably did this when you used the K-W-L strategy.)

As you read this selection, circle words or phrases that are unfamiliar to you, including tough vocabulary or things that you just don't know about. Make notes by places where you read more slowly, reread, or stopped to ask a question.

from **"A Personal Narrative"** by Kim-Hue Phan

Response notes

I was born in Saigon, and I escaped from Vietnam four years ago. I'm seventeen now and in the eleventh grade in an American school.

When I left home, Saigon was in bad shape; it was not pretty like it was before 1975. We didn't have a house in the city anymore. After the war was over in 1975, we lived outside the city, and I was really lucky to stay in school. I usually got up at 5:00 A.M., cooked breakfast for the family, cleaned the house and went to school from 7:00 A.M. to noon. After school, I cooked lunch and cared for the family. I promised my parents to take care of all my younger brothers and sisters. If everything went okay, then I could stay in school. My father drove a bus to different cities; my mother went along with my father to buy merchandise to sell to the black market in Saigon. My sister worked at a factory.

School in Saigon was hard. Mostly we read books and took tests. Children had to memorize a long poem or essay every day. Most of the teachers were really mean; I was spanked because I couldn't memorize a poem. After 1975, the rule was that teachers should not punish the kids, but I was spanked because I did not write a five-page essay about flowers in a basket. My father protested, and the teacher didn't spank me after that.

from **"A Personal Narrative"** by Kim-Hue Phan

In seventh grade in Saigon, we had to read hero stories a lot. After 1975, the communists took over the country and republished all our books. Their stories were about heroes who spied for the North Vietnamese. We usually read a biography of Ho Chi Minh. I used to go to the library to borrow the books. The communists didn't allow non-communist books in libraries. They allowed only books published by the communists, like hero stories or biographies of Viet Cong. I was forced to read these communists' stories. Many people were against the communists but were afraid to say anything against them.

✏ Was this selection difficult to read? Why or why not?

....

....

....

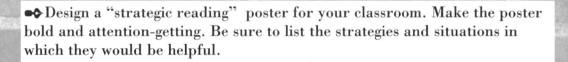

✏ Design a "strategic reading" poster for your classroom. Make the poster bold and attention-getting. Be sure to list the strategies and situations in which they would be helpful.

When you encounter challenges in your reading, try changing pace, rereading, or reading on.

Four
Putting Words in Context

What do you do if you come across a word you don't know while reading? One way to figure out challenging words is to look at the **context,** the other words around an unknown word. The context can provide important clues to help you figure out the meaning of an unknown word. Read this sentence and see if you can figure out the meaning of the italicized word:

> One of the boys was very brave, but the other was *timorous.*

Think it through:
The word <u>but</u> in the sentence means that two things are different, so <u>timorous</u> must be the opposite of <u>brave</u>. <u>Timorous</u> probably means "fearful" or "scared."

Once you think you know the meaning of the word, replace the unknown word in the sentence with what you think it means. Does your "new" sentence make sense? If you're still uncertain, you can always check the meaning in a dictionary.

As you read this article, circle or highlight any words that are unfamiliar to you. Try to use context clues to figure out what the words mean.

from *An Owl in the House* by Alice Calaprice

Response notes

A few years ago I did something that I probably shouldn't have done, but to my mind I didn't have much of a choice, really. I adopted a wild animal—a baby great horned owl—after I found it buried in the snow in the Vermont woods near my home.

I am a zoologist and naturalist. That means I study animals that live in the wild. I know very well that wild animals should usually be left to fend for themselves, and that many die an early death in the process. This is the way nature intended it to be. It is unkind to force a wild animal into captivity. Tampering with nature's ways causes the natural system of interdependence of all wild animals and plants to become unbalanced. In addition, most wild animals die when they leave their natural habitat and food supply. Despite this knowledge, I felt a moment of kinship with the owlet and instinctively reached out to protect it. I could not leave it there to die.

Most wild animals are protected by government agencies, and it is illegal to take them as pets. But I knew that, because I am a scientist, I could get permission to keep the owl and to study its development. I was very curious about how a docile owlet develops into a large and fierce predator; I was also curious about how this owl would interact with human beings.

from *An Owl in the House* by Alice Calaprice

←Response notes

Male and female owlets look alike, so for no particular reason I decided to refer to this one as "he." I named him Bubo, which is part of his scientific name, *bubo virginianus*. Bubo become very special to me, and I think I was special to him.

●❖Write the words you circled in the chart below; then go back to the selection and use context to figure out what each word means. First look at all the words in the sentence and paragraph around the unknown word. Underline or circle any words that give you clues about the meaning of each unfamiliar word. Then write what you think the word means.

Words I Don't Know	Word Meanings

124

Share your chart with a partner. Explain how you used the strategy of using context to figure out what the words mean. Here is an example of how you might explain:

> I did not know exactly what the word <u>captivity</u> means. I reread the sentence, and it said that it is not kind to force a wild animal into captivity. If you are forcing a person or an animal to do something, that means you want him or her to do something he or she usually wouldn't do. So <u>captivity</u> must be the opposite of <u>wild</u>. I think that <u>captivity</u> means "locked up" or "not free."

●◆ Play a game using context. Make up two nonsense words and write "dictionary" meanings for the words. Then write each word in a sentence. Be sure your sentences have enough context so that a reader can figure out what the nonsense words mean. Trade sentences with a partner and see how close you can come to the "real" meanings of each other's nonsense words.

Nonsense Word 1: ....

"Dictionary" Meaning:

Nonsense Word 2: ....

"Dictionary" Meaning:

125

Sentence 1:

Sentence 2:

To figure out the meaning of a word you don't know, read the word or words around the unknown word.

Using **context clues** is one strategy for figuring out what words mean. You can also use **structural clues** to figure out meaning. Think of words as being made of building blocks—each block, or word part, can provide a clue to meaning. For example, a reader is someone who reads. If you reread something, you read it again. How are *reader* and *reread* the same? Both have the same basic building block—the root word *read*. But one word uses the suffix *-er*, which means "someone who," and the other uses the prefix *re-*, which means "do again."

The following article about Leonardo da Vinci, a famous painter, inventor, and scientist, has some pretty long and complicated-looking words in it. As you read, circle words that are unfamiliar to you. Try to figure out what the words mean by separating them into parts. Look for the root word to help you figure out the meaning. You can write out the parts or "building blocks" in the response notes. This chart of word parts might help you:

Word Part	Meaning
-able	that can be done; deserving to be
astro-	about stars, planets, or space
circum-	in a circle around
eco-	about the environment
-er, -or	someone who
fore-	coming before
-ist	person who does or makes
-less	without something
-ness	state of being something (happiness, state of being happy)
ped-	having to do with the feet
pre-	done before
re-	again or once more

"Leonardo da Vinci" from *Experimenting with Inventions*
by Robert Gardner

← Response notes →

For centuries the world has regarded Leonardo da Vinci (1452–1519) as one of the world's greatest painters. The faces we see in his *Mona Lisa* and *Last Supper* are amazingly real. Leonardo's notebooks, discovered in this century in old libraries, reveal that Leonardo was more than a great painter.

"Leonardo da Vinci" from *Experimenting with Inventions*
by Robert Gardner

Response notes

He was an inventor, architect, botanist, ecologist, astronomer, mathematician, and anatomist.

Unfortunately for the world, Leonardo kept his ideas to himself. His notebooks are written in print that can be read only with a mirror. Did he fear the wrath of other scholars who held different opinions? Or was he keeping his findings secret until that day when he would at last understand the grand designs of nature?

We now doubt he wrote in mirror image form in order to keep his ideas secret. Rather, because he was left-handed he probably found it easier to write from right to left.

His inventions, which were drawn in great detail in his notebooks, were often centuries ahead of their time. For example, he invented a four-wheel horseless wagon powered by two giant springs that were to be alternately wound by a "conductor" using a lever. Recognizing that wheels would have to turn at different speeds on curves, he circumvented the need for a differential by supplying power to only one wheel. His car was the forerunner of today's toy wind-up cars. Why don't we find spring-powered cars on today's highways?

He invented a wooden tank for warfare. The tank, made of heavy planks, had a cannon on each side, in front, and in back. It was mounted on four wheels powered by cranks turned by men inside. He invented a diving suit that would allow a diver to breathe air stored in a wineskin as he made his way to the bottom of the hull of an enemy ship. Once there, he could cut holes in the ship causing it to sink.

Some of his other inventions include a movable cam, a ratchet jack, a device for measuring the strength of wires, a machine for rolling copper and tin into sheets, a monkey wrench, a pair of pliers, a reciprocating saw, a pipe borer, a device for automatically feeding paper into printing presses, a needle grinder to mass-produce needles, a pedometer, a machine for stamping coins, a device for measuring wind speed, a worm gear, a pump to force water from deep wells or mines, a floating dredge to clear swamps, and a type of prefabricated housing. He developed cord drives. In his notebook he wrote, "Every motion machine with cords is quieter than one that is made with toothed wheels and pinions." He thus anticipated today's belt-driven machines. Da Vinci was surely an inventor ahead of his time!

127

●◆Look back at the article to see what words you circled or highlighted. Write the words in the chart below. Then use word parts to figure out what the words mean. (Some of the words may not have word parts that you can figure out—in that case, use context clues to decide what the words mean.)

Words I Don't Know	Word Meanings

128

Figure out the meaning of an unfamiliar word by breaking the word into parts and determining what the parts mean.

Active Reading: Social Studies

Visit an ancient pyramid . . . sail down the Nile River . . . trade for goods at an Egyptian market-place . . . study how to write hiero-glyphics at scribe school. Did you know you could do all these things just by reading a *textbook*?

Textbooks (and other nonfiction writing) are full of fascinating facts and great adventures. This unit will help you get the most out of your reading by teaching you some strategies for reading textbooks, such as previewing, paraphrasing, and taking notes. You'll learn how to make facts "come alive" by getting involved in what you're reading. And you just might uncover a few fascinating facts about ancient Egypt along the way.

One

Coming Attractions

Movie theaters often run previews before the featured film—short "clips" that tell you about coming attractions. Imagine if these previews showed almost entire movies. Not only would you be at the theater for hours, but it would also take away the fun of seeing the films. A preview usually gives you just enough information to get you interested in a movie without giving away all of the details.

Just as a coming attraction gives you a glimpse of a new movie, a preview of a textbook chapter can tell you what to expect without revealing everything that's in the chapter. **Previewing** is <u>not</u> reading the whole chapter. Instead, it's taking a little time to get to know the subject and to try to figure out what you should look for as you read. Here are some previewing tips:

✔ Read the title first.

✔ Read headings and subheadings.

✔ Look at photos, illustrations, and other graphics.

✔ Read all the photo and illustration captions.

Preview this textbook chapter about ancient Egypt. As you read the title and first section, think like a detective. Circle any information that gives you clues about what this chapter will be about.

130

≡RESPONSE NOTES≡

from *World: Adventures in Time and Place*

READ ALOUD

"Hail O Nile, who comes to give life to the people of Egypt. Created by the sun-god to give life to all who thirst. Who lets the desert drink with streams descending from heaven. Who makes barley and creates wheat so that temples celebrate. When the Nile overflows, offerings are made to you, cattle are [killed] for you, that your goodness be repaid."

These words are from a 3,000-year-old Egyptian song, "Hymn to the Nile."

➥ What do you think the focus of this chapter will be? Why?

....

....

....

....

Now preview the entire chapter. Remember that your goal is not to read all the words. Instead, look at titles and subtitles, ideas in bold letters, and so on. In the response notes, write down some key questions that you think this chapter will answer.

from *World: Adventures in Time and Place*

RESPONSE NOTES

THE BIG PICTURE

Around 5000 B.C. people began building farming villages in a river valley in Africa, several hundred miles south of Catal Huyuk. The area around Egypt's **Nile River** valley probably did not look like a very good place to start farming.

The river wound its way through a vast desert with few signs of life. Yet every year the Nile flooded its banks. The river swamped everything in its path with water and mud for four solid months—from July through October.

This yearly flood made the Nile Valley lush and green. It also allowed people to make use of the land. With the help of water from the Nile River, ancient farmers turned the Nile Valley into a productive agricultural region.

THE GIFT OF THE NILE

In many ways, Egyptian civilization owes its life to the Nile River. The Nile provided water and food in the desert. This seemed like a blessing from the gods of the ancient people. For that reason, Egypt has often been called the "Gift of the Nile."

A Mighty River

The Nile is the world's longest river. It flows over 4,000 miles north from the snowcapped mountains of East Africa. It passes through the present-day countries of Uganda, Ethiopia, Sudan, and Egypt. Then the Nile empties into the warm Mediterranean Sea.

Much of East Africa has a rainy season that lasts from May until September. During that time the Nile swells with rainwater and rushes northward with extra power. The river carries off silt as it goes. Silt is a mixture of tiny bits of soil and rock.

Over time, much of the silt has been deposited where the Nile empties into the Mediterranean. There the river divides into several branches, forming a vast, fan-shaped **delta**. A delta is very fertile, flat land made of silt left behind as a river drains into a larger body of water.

The Nile Delta region is in northern Egypt, and appears nearer the top on maps that have north at the top. This makes the Delta seem to be "higher." However, the Delta is called **Lower Egypt,** because it is the lower, or downstream, part of the Nile.

← Response notes →

In **Upper Egypt,** to the south, the Nile cuts through stone cliffs and desert sands. This landscape is very different from the mild, fertile Delta.

A LAND OF DROUGHT AND FLOOD

Egyptian farmers almost always welcomed the mud left by each summer's Nile flood. This silt-filled mud was rich in minerals needed by plants. The black soil brought by the Nile contrasted sharply with the dry, yellow sand of Egypt's desert. In many places a farmer could stand with one foot on farmland and the other on sand!

Farmers depended on the right amount of flooding each year to grow successful crops. Too little flooding meant farmers' crops failed and people went hungry. Too much meant people and cattle could be swept away and homes destroyed. Life was a delicate balance in the Nile River valley.

A System of Agriculture

In October the flooded land began to dry. Then farmers planted wheat and barley. They also planted garden vegetables such as cucumbers, lettuce, onions, and beans. Farmers also grew flax, a plant used to make cloth.

To water their newly planted crops, Egypt's farmers used a form of technology called **irrigation.** Irrigation is the watering of land by means of canals or pipes. At first, farmers simply built dirt walls around their farmland to hold the Nile floodwaters in the fields. Later, they dug small channels, or canals, to bring water from the Nile directly to their farmland. Farmers scooped water from the canals and poured it into the fields, using a bucket-lifter called a shadouf (shah DOOF). This tool is still used today.

By March the crops were ready for harvesting. In good years the fields were filled with ripe vegetables and grains. Then farm families had more food than they needed. Their surplus, or extra supply of goods, was then gathered up and carried off to storehouses. As in Catal Huyuk, these grain stores made specialization and community life possible.

Travel Along the Nile

Harvest-time ended in late June, before the Nile once again began to flood. During the four-month flood season, farmers could not work in their fields. Instead, many used the time to visit neighboring villages.

Flood season was one of the busiest times for travel on the Nile. Yet river traffic was heavy all year. The Nile was the main way that people and goods moved from place to place. The 600-mile journey between Upper and Lower Egypt would take over a month to walk. In a reed boat it took only about half that time.

132

●◆Based on your previewing, what details would you expect to find about the Nile in this chapter? Make a web to show what you expect.

The Nile has a flood season.

Nile River

133

●◆With a partner, create a previewing game for younger students. What rules should you follow to preview a chapter? How do you win the game? Write a set of directions. Use the directions to play "The Preview Game" with a chapter from your own social studies textbook.

The Preview Game
Rules:
1.

2.

3.

To Win the Game:

Preview a chapter of a textbook to get an idea of what the chapter is about and how it is organized.

Two It's What's Important That Counts

Another strategy for reading a textbook is to **highlight** important ideas. Highlighting not only helps you get involved in what you're reading, it also helps you remember information. To highlight, underline or circle the information that you think is most important.

As you read the following paragraphs, ask yourself: "What are the main points the author is trying to make?" Then highlight the most important ideas by circling the main points about medicine and science in Egypt.

← Response notes

from *World: Adventures in Time and Place*

Medicine in Egypt

Most Egyptian doctors were actually priests who learned their skills in temple schools. The storehouse of medical knowledge in temple schools was vast and old. For thousands of years priests had noted different kinds of illnesses and injuries and what worked best in treating them. When writing was invented, scribes wrote down this knowledge. The world's first medical textbooks were born! The medical books told doctors how to cure illnesses, stitch together cuts, and set broken bones. The books also explained how to "measure the heart" to see if it was beating too quickly or slowly. Do you know how to measure your own pulse?

Many ancient Egyptian cures centered around treatments that are no longer used. Many other cures, however, introduced ingredients that we still use today. Chamomile, an herb used to make tea, was used to calm upset stomachs. Moldy bread was often placed on wounds. This sounds terrible until we remember that modern antibiotics, or germ-killing drugs, are often made from certain kinds of molds!

Math and Science

Along with medicine, Egyptian priests knew a great deal about mathematics. They developed the mathematical rules needed in building the pyramids, for example.

The priest-scientists also used their knowledge of math to understand the stars. Without telescopes, Egyptians identified five of the solar system's planets, which they called the "stars that know no rest." The mysterious darkness of eclipses did not scare priests. They had figured out that such events were just "meetings of the Sun and Moon."

●◆ Look back at the information that you highlighted. Imagine that you are in charge of a museum exhibit about ancient Egypt. Use the ideas you highlighted to make a sign for a display called "The Egyptians—Doctors and Scientists."

135

●◆ Now read the chapter about the Nile in Lesson One. Highlight the most important ideas by circling them as you read. Then ask yourself: "How did highlighting help me understand what I read?" Explain your answer.

Highlighting helps you identify and remember the most important information.

© GREAT SOURCE. ALL RIGHTS RESERVED.

Three

Keeping Track

If you've ever had to write a research report, you probably read about your topic in several different places, like encyclopedias, magazine articles, and the Internet. But how did you keep track of all the facts? One way to organize information as you read is by taking notes—writing down information about the topic. Like highlighting, taking notes keeps you actively involved in your reading and helps you remember what you read. But notes are usually a little more detailed than **highlighting**. Rather than just writing down the **main ideas**, you also write details about them. A few tips about note-taking:

> ✓ Notes do not need to be in complete sentences. You can jot down words or phrases.
>
> ✓ There is no one right way to take notes. Some people make formal outlines or lists, while other people use webs or other graphic organizers. Pick a style that works for you.
>
> ✓ Don't take notes about everything that you read. Write only the most important ideas.
>
> ✓ Organize your notes with headings, titles, or whatever system works for you.
>
> ✓ Use numbers, symbols, and/or abbreviations to help you take notes more quickly.

Imagine that you are an archaeologist, studying one of the most fascinating topics in ancient Egypt—mummies. As you read the excerpt, jot down some notes in the response notes.

← Response notes

from *The Ancient Egyptians* by Elsa Marston

Why did the ancient Egyptians mummify their dead? The procedure was an essential part of their belief in the afterlife. For a person to enjoy eternal life, his or her body had to be preserved.

The Egyptians probably got the idea by observing that desert sands would sometimes dry and preserve a body naturally. Then they learned how to mummify artificially. Though at first only the royal and rich had the privilege of being preserved, later almost everyone but the very poor expected to be mummified. There were different grades of mummification, from the quick, cheap job to the full seventy days' treatment for kings.

136

from ***The Ancient Egyptians*** by Elsa Marston

The first step in mummification was to take out most of the internal organs and preserve them. The heart was left in the body to be weighed by the gods; the brain, though, was discarded because it was not thought to be of any value. After being immersed for many days in a special kind of salt called natron, the body was treated with special ointments and finally wrapped carefully in long strips of linen. The mummification business was always a thriving one, and it lasted well into Roman times.

●◆ Sometimes it helps to use a graphic organizer to keep track of information. Review your notes. Then use this sequence map to organize information about the steps involved in mummification.

1. Internal organs were taken out and preserved.

2.

3.

4.

5.

6.

➤ Now reread the chapter on the Nile in Lesson One. Review the information you highlighted. Use your highlighting and any notes you've made to write a short magazine article about the Nile.

Taking
notes as you read
is another way to help you
organize and remember
important ideas.

Four

To Sum Up

Another strategy for reading textbooks and other informational writing is to summarize what you read. **Summarizing**, or briefly restating the main ideas in your own words, helps you understand and remember the most important information.

As you read the information about pyramids, highlight the ideas that you think are most important. In the response notes, jot down notes about what you are reading.

from **Egyptian Pyramids** by Anne Steel

Response notes

FAMOUS PYRAMIDS

The earliest Egyptian graves were very simple and could easily be broken into and robbed. To prevent this, the Egyptians began to build tombs called mastabas. These were rectangular buildings placed over a burial chamber. Pharaohs had mastabas built with many rooms inside to protect the burial chamber from thieves, but the graves were still robbed.

The first pyramid was built for Pharaoh Zoser at Sakkara. There were six huge steps built on top of the tomb to make it safer from robbers. The Pharaoh's spirit was believed to have climbed the steps of the pyramid to the stars. Later pyramids were built without steps, like the famous group at Giza. The largest of these is the Great Pyramid, built for Pharaoh Khufu. Each side is 450 feet (144 m) high and measures 756 feet (230 m) at the base. It would have taken at least twenty years to build.

THE PYRAMID BUILDERS

Many thousands of people were needed to build a pyramid. Some of them, such as the architect and planners, were highly skilled. Their plans had to be accepted by the pharaoh before any work could begin. Quarry men were needed to get the stone out of the ground, and masons worked to shape the rough stone. Painters decorated the walls inside the tomb, and sculptors made statues and carvings.

The heavy work of moving the stones was done by people with no special building skills. Some of them were farmers who had to leave their land for some time each year when the Nile flooded. Others may have been prisoners, or people paying labor tax to the pharaoh. As there was no money in Ancient Egypt, the workers were paid with food, wine, clothes and other goods.

●◆Use your notes to write a summary of the selection.

....

....

....

....

....

....

....

●◆Now use your summary to design a "trading card" about pyramids. Include a sketch of a pyramid on one side, and interesting facts from your summary on the other.

Summarizing helps you understand and remember what you read.

Five

Graphs, Maps, and More

A map helps you see the best way to get where you're going. A picture of clouds and rain in the newspaper tells you the forecast for the day. A time line shows you that the car was invented after the airplane. In all of these cases, you are using **graphic sources**—pictures that communicate ideas. Social studies materials use many different types of graphic sources, such as maps, charts, diagrams, and pie graphs. When you come across one of these graphics, try to figure out how it relates to the text. Use it to help you better understand what you are reading.

Look at the diagram of the pyramid. As you read the excerpt that goes with it, draw lines from the parts of the diagram to the sentences that describe those particular parts.

from *Egyptian Pyramids* by Anne Steel

Response notes

The pharoah's burial chamber

Ante-chamber

The grand gallery

The corridor blocked by huge stone slabs

The entrance to the pyramid

False burial chamber

The main passages inside a pyramid, showing false passageways and dead ends.

Inside, the pyramid was a maze of passages and rooms. The main aim of the builders was to hide the burial chamber so that thieves could not steal its treasures. The entrance was usually on the north side of the pyramid and it was always well hidden. Inside, the passages might lead to false burial chambers or dead ends. In the Great Pyramid there was a false chamber underground. The real chamber was blocked off with huge stone slabs. But this was not enough to keep robbers from stealing everything except the stone tomb.

●✦As you read the description and looked at the diagram, how were you able to figure out the purpose of each part of the pyramid? How did the diagram help you understand pyramids better?

....

....

....

....

●✦Create a graphic to go with one of the other pieces of writing in this unit. Use your imagination, but remember that your graphic should be helpful to a reader. Here are some ideas to help you get started:

• A diagram of the Nile River with drawings that show the uses of the river by the ancient Egyptians

• A flow chart that explains the process of making a mummy

Graphic
sources
can help
you "see"
what
you're
reading.

Active Reading: Expository Writing

Active readers know how important it is to become involved in a piece of writing. This is especially true when you read expository nonfiction.

Expository nonfiction is writing that explains. It is the front page of your local newspaper, the top story on your six o'clock news, and the first chapter of your social studies book. Expository nonfiction is the truth—or at least one person's version of the truth.

But, as you'll discover in this unit, along with all the facts, expository nonfiction can also tell stories—like the story of the *Titanic* or a story about the day it rained frogs.

Finding the Main Idea

Active readers know that to understand a piece of expository **nonfiction**, they must first understand its main idea. The **main idea** is the most important idea of a piece of writing. Sometimes a writer will be very direct in stating the main idea. Other times a writer will leave it to the reader to make **inferences** (reasonable guesses) about the main idea. To find the main idea, look at the subject of the writing—the person, place, or thing the author is writing about. Ask yourself: What does the author have to say about the subject? This is the main idea.

Read the excerpt from *Can It Really Rain Frogs?* by weather forecaster Spencer Christian. As you read, circle words that relate to the subject of the article. Underline words that relate to the main idea.

response notes

144

from *Can It Really Rain Frogs?* by Spencer Christian

Just before eight o'clock one Thursday morning in October 1947, a man named A. D. Bajkov and his wife were having breakfast at a restaurant in Marksville, Louisiana, when the waitress came over to their table and made an odd announcement: "Fish are falling from the sky!"

Mr. and Mrs. Bajkov rushed outside to see what all the excitement was about. Sure enough, covering the streets, roofs, and yards, and hanging in the trees of the small town were thousands of fresh fish, flapping about in the morning fog.

When we say "It's raining cats and dogs," we don't mean that Garfields and Lassies are falling from the sky—it's just an expression we use to describe heavy rain. But it really did rain fish on that morning in 1947. How could this happen?

No one has ever observed snakes, frogs, fish, or other animals being carried up into the skies. The only logical explanation for these strange rains, however, is that the culprits are *tornadoes*, columns of air that drop down from storm clouds and twirl at very high speed, or *waterspouts*, tornadoes that touch down on water instead of land. There are numerous accounts of tornadoes picking up trucks, automobiles, farm equipment, even entire houses, and depositing them elsewhere.

Large waterspouts have been reported picking up objects as big as a five-ton houseboat, so it makes sense that they could pick up small creatures like fish and frogs. Once aloft, the living debris could be carried tens, perhaps hundreds, of miles by powerful winds before plummeting to Earth in the downdrafts of a thunderstorm, or dropped when the wind died down.

There have also been accounts in ancient writings of red, yellow, and milk-white downpours, sometimes described as rains of blood or milk. These rains were probably colored by

from *Can It Really Rain Frogs?* by Spencer Christian

small particles of dust or plant pollen that had been blown
great distances. The Sahara Desert contains areas of reddish
iron dust picked up by desert whirlwinds, and in some areas
red algae grows so quickly after a storm that it seems as if it
fell from the sky. Yellow rains result when certain tree pollens
are blown upwards. And gray volcanic ash blown into the sky
mixes with water to form a white rain that looks like milk.

●◆ Draw a story board or comic strip that shows Christian's main idea. Your
story board or comic strip should focus on the message Christian wants to
send to readers. For example, if you think Christian's main idea has to do
with the weird and wacky side of weather, you might draw a comic strip with
two people who are looking up at the sky and saying something funny about
the weather. Use the notes you made while reading to help you come up with
ideas for your art.

Recognizing
the main idea of a piece helps
you understand what the piece
is all about.

Two
Dealing with Details

Active readers pay close attention to the details a writer uses. **Details** are words an author uses to describe, to persuade an audience or explain a process, or to support the main idea. Details are important to expository writing because they:

- Support the main idea
- Make the writing interesting to read

Details are "helpers" for the main idea in the same way that your fingers are "helpers" for your hand. Details can make a main idea work effectively, just as your fingers make your hand work effectively. Of course, a writer can't just stuff five-fingers' worth of details into a piece of writing and leave it at that. The details the writer uses need to be vivid and memorable.

Reread *Can It Really Rain Frogs?* Pay close attention to the details that support Christian's main idea. Note five of these details—one for each finger—on the hand below. On the palm of the hand, write a sentence or two that explains Christian's main idea.

146

Detail:

Detail:

Detail:

Main Idea:

Detail:

Detail:

●◆Now prepare to write an expository piece on a subject you know a lot about. Get ready by filling in a "main idea/detail hand" on your subject.

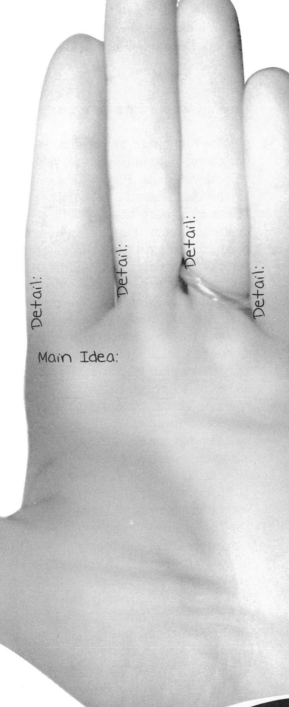

Detail:

Detail:

Detail:

Detail:

Main Idea:

Detail:

Writers use details to support the main idea and to make their writing more interesting.

Expository nonfiction can be organized in many ways. Some expository writers write in time-order **sequence**. This means that the writer tells about the events in the order they happened. As you read this excerpt from *The Titanic*, pay particular attention to the sequence of events that led up to one of the worst seafaring disasters ever. Also highlight any transitional words you find, such as *then, next,* and *later*. (Writers use words like these to help their readers keep track of the sequence.)

← Response notes →

from ***The Titanic*** by Richard Wormser

The night was bitter cold. Stars shone like diamonds in the dark sky, but there was no moon. The water was calm, and smooth as glass. High in the crow's nest, two young sailors, Frederick Fleet and Herbert Lee, were watching for icebergs. These men were the "eyes of the ship"—part of the team of lookouts. From their perch above the *Titanic's* deck, they could gaze far out into the open sea and spot any danger before it seriously threatened the ship. Radar and other electronic scanning devices had not yet been invented, so watching closely was the only way to spot objects in the water. But these lookouts didn't even have a pair of binoculars.

By 11:30 P.M., most passengers were in bed. Fleet and Lee were glad their shift would be over in another 20 minutes. They were numb with cold and their eyes hurt from the strain of trying to see in the dark. Then at 11:39 P.M., Fleet suddenly spied an object which at first seemed small but rapidly increased in size. Within seconds he realized that the *Titanic* was headed straight for an iceberg. He snatched up the telephone and rang the bridge, the officer's control center. As soon as the officer answered, Fleet cried out:

"Iceberg dead ahead!"

The great ship was about to meet her fate.

It only took 37 seconds for the *Titanic* to begin its swing away from the 100-foot-high, 500-foot-deep iceberg in its path. To lookouts Fleet and Lee, that was way too long. It seemed certain that the *Titanic* would crash head-on into the mountain of ice. William Murdoch, the first officer in charge, had already given orders to change the ship's course. A ship as large as the *Titanic*, however, needed time to reposition. Fifteen seconds more and the *Titanic* would have escaped. But time was the one thing the *Titanic* didn't have.

The *Titanic* was about to crash into the iceberg when it suddenly began to swerve out of the iceberg's path. To the officers on the bridge, it seemed that their last-minute attempts to change course had worked. The ship appeared to have only

from ***The Titanic*** by Richard Wormser

lightly scraped the iceberg. But many passengers and crew below were aware that something much more serious had happened.

Response notes

●◆What is the sequence of events that Wormser describes? Use the diagram below to show what happened first, what happened next, and so on.

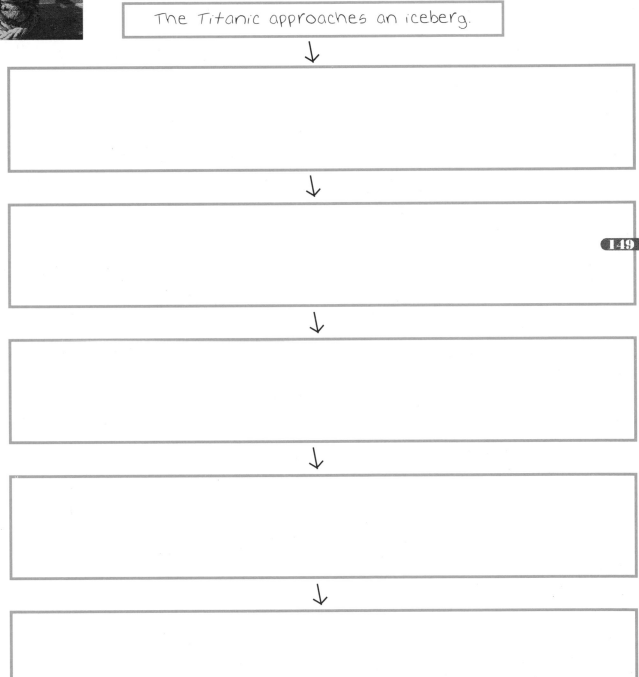

The *Titanic* approaches an iceberg.

↓

↓

↓

↓

↓

➥Now imagine you are the investigating officer assigned to review the events leading up to the *Titanic* disaster. Examine the sequence of events. Then write an "official" report in which you answer this question: Could the *Titanic* disaster have been avoided?

Official Report

Prepared by:

Understanding sequence helps you keep track of information.

Four

Considering Cause and Effect

Cause and effect is another way to organize expository nonfiction. A **cause-and-effect** relationship means that one event (the cause) brings on the other event (the effect). Paying attention to causes and effects helps you connect events and ideas as you read.

Read another excerpt from *The Titanic*. As you read, highlight possible causes of the disaster.

from ***The Titanic*** by Richard Wormser

Four crew members relaxing in a first-class lounge heard a grinding noise from deep inside the ship. It sounded, one said, as if "a propeller had fallen off." Many first-class passengers felt a shock. To Marguerite Frolicher, a young Swiss woman, it seemed, "as if the ship were landing." Lady Duff Gordon, a dress designer married to a British nobleman, commented that it was as if "someone had run a giant finger along the side of the ship."

On the ship's lower decks, the noise was even louder. Some people in second class were awakened by the jolt. Major Arthur Godfrey Peuchen, a Canadian, thought "a heavy wave" had struck the ship. Mrs. Walter Stephenson, who had lived through the 1906 San Francisco earthquake, thought the shock felt like an earthquake tremor.

Deep within the ship, the men tending the boilers that powered the *Titanic* knew exactly what had happened. In one of the boiler rooms, a tremendous rumbling, scraping sound was heard, followed by a terrifying roar as tons of sea water came crashing into the ship. The whole left side of the ship seemed to collapse suddenly. The men barely escaped with their lives.

In the third-class area, Carl Bohme, a Finnish immigrant, got out of bed to see what was going on and found himself up to his ankles in water. In the mailroom, the water was already covering the knees of the postal workers, who were frantically trying to keep the mail from getting wet.

Most passengers still didn't realize how serious things were. Some third-class passengers had discovered that their deck was covered with ice that had fallen from the iceberg. Some began to have a snowball fight. Soon passengers from every class were picking up pieces of ice. Some even used the ice to cool

Response notes

151

from *The Titanic* by Richard Wormser

← Response notes

their drinks. Whatever the problem, they seemed confident that it would soon be solved.

A few passengers, however, were well aware that something was terribly wrong. Lawrence Beasley, a schoolteacher traveling in second class, had started back to his cabin when he noticed that somehow his feet weren't falling in the right place. The stairs were level, but he felt slightly off balance. It was as if the steps were suddenly tilting forward toward the *bow*, the front part of the ship. In fact, they were.

Below the decks was Thomas Andrews, the chief engineer who had supervised the design of the *Titanic*. He was on board to see how the ship would perform on her maiden voyage and whether any adjustments needed to be made. No one knew the *Titanic* better than Andrews. No man, not even Captain Smith, commanded more respect from the crew. Now the ship's officers were anxiously waiting for him to tell them what was happening.

Andrews studied the reports of the damage and then gave Captain Smith the bad news: The rock-hard base of the iceberg had scraped the *Titanic*'s hull below the waterline, gashing some holes in her side and loosening the steel plates that held her together. Water was rushing into the front of the ship. Andrews explained there were 16 water-tight compartments on the ship from bow to *stern*, the back end of the ship. The ship could float if the first four were filled. But if the fifth compartment, or bulkhead, was filled, the bow would begin to sink so low that water would spill over that bulkhead into the sixth compartment. Because the *Titanic*'s bulkheads were not high enough to prevent this from happening, the spillover would continue from compartment to compartment until the whole ship filled with water and sank.

The *Titanic* was doomed.

"How long have we got?" the captain asked.

"About two hours," Andrews replied.

Smith and Andrews both knew that there were 2,207 passengers and crew on board, but room for only about 1,178 people in the lifeboats. Unless a rescue ship arrived within two hours, more than 1,000 people would drown. There was no time to waste.

●◆ On the diagram below, list some of the causes of the *Titanic* disaster.

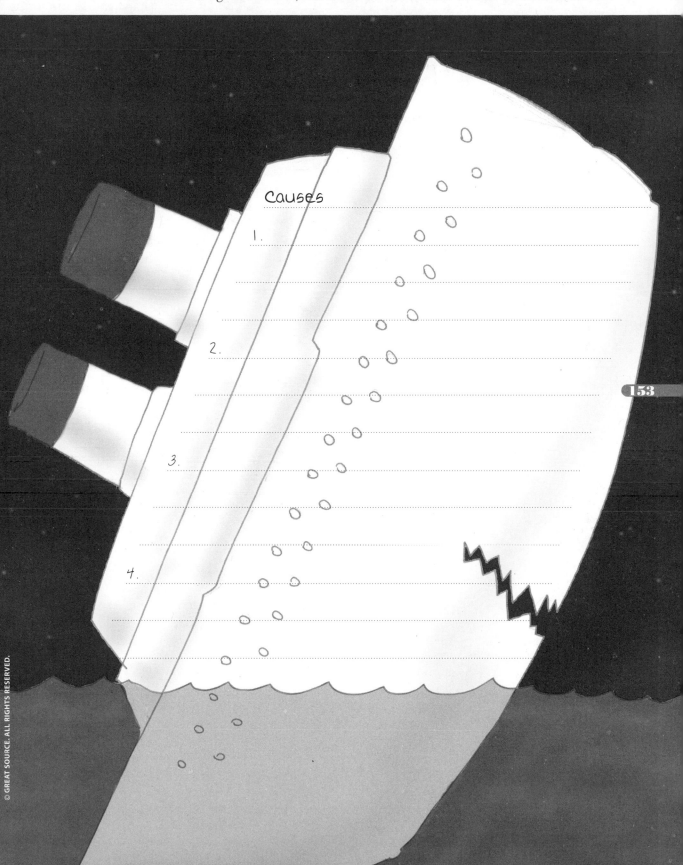

Causes

1. ....

....

....

2. ....

....

....

3. ....

....

....

4. ....

....

....

153

➡ Use your diagram to help you write the next part of your "official" report: what <u>caused</u> the *Titanic* disaster.

Official Report

Prepared by: ....

....

....

....

....

....

....

....

....

154

....

....

....

....

....

....

....

....

....

Recognizing cause and effect relationships helps you connect events and ideas.

Five

Investigating and Inferring

Active readers need to be able to read a line, a paragraph, or a page of expository nonfiction and then make **inferences** (reasonable guesses) about the meaning of the writing.

Read this excerpt from *It's Our World, Too!*, a nonfiction book about real kids who have accomplished amazing things. Notice the examples of inferences in the response notes. As you read, add other inferences of your own in the margin.

from ***It's Our World, Too!*** by Phillip Hoose

One day Sarah Rosen's sixth-grade teacher announced that their school would be reenacting the Constitutional Convention of 1787. But, he said, only boys could take part since only men had participated in the convention. Sarah was <u>furious</u>, but she seemed to be the only one who cared enough to do anything about it. How could one girl change the whole school?

At <u>first</u> it sounded like a great idea to Sarah Rosen and her classmates in Mr. Starczewski's sixth grade class. Students at the Muessel School in South Bend, Indiana, would reenact the Constitutional Convention of 1787, where delegates from twelve of the thirteen new states drew up and signed the U.S. Constitution.

Mr. Star—that's what everyone called their teacher— explained that each of the fourth, fifth, and sixth grade classes would be a state. Students in each class would elect delegates, who would dress up in costumes of the time and pretend to be the original delegates to the convention. Mr. Star said that their class would be South Carolina, and that they would elect four delegates.

Sarah looked around the room, measuring her chances to be elected. There were twenty-one students in her class, ten girls and eleven boys. She was well known and liked, but so were plenty of others. Well, maybe, she thought.

And then Mr. Star dropped the bomb. "Half the class isn't going to like this," he said. "But only boys can be delegates, and only boys will be allowed to vote for delegates."

Sarah felt tears beginning to build as she raised her hand. "Why can't girls be delegates?"

Mr. Star explained that the teachers wanted the event to be as close to history as possible. Since there had been no women delegates back then in Philadelphia, he said, there would be no girl delegates now at Muessel School.

Sarah hated discrimination of any kind. She didn't care

Response notes

mad because girls not included

Why wasn't anyone else mad?

must have **155** changed their minds later

what had happened two hundred years ago. To her, this was just plain discrimination against girls. Besides, nearly half the boys in the school, and in her class, were black or Asian or Hispanic. Two hundred years ago, they would have been left out, too. The black boys would have been slaves, without the right to vote, and Hispanics and Asians hadn't immigrated to the United States yet. But at Muessel, only girls were going to be left out. What did that say about how her teacher felt about the rights of women?

Sarah wanted to say a million things at once, but she knew she didn't speak well when she was angry. She waited for the bell to ring, then rushed past her friends to her locker and boarded the bus.

She was already crying by the time she got home. "Sarah, what's wrong?" her mother said. She wiped her tears on her sleeve and told the story. The telling itself seemed to clear her head. And an idea came: she would organize a counter-demonstration of the girls in her class. Let the boys walk around in costumes and pretend to be delegates if they wanted. The girls would take to the halls, chanting and singing in protest. They would represent the women the Constitution forgot back in 1787.

There wasn't much time to lose. It was Friday night, and the mock convention was scheduled for the next Wednesday. Sarah picked up the phone and called the classmates she thought she could count on the most, Jennifer Spinsky and the Wiand sisters, Betsy and Jennifer. They were angry, too. One idea led to another—signs they could make, songs they could sing. They made up chants and slogans.

When Sarah hung up, her mother took the phone and called the principal, Dr. Calvin, to object as a parent to the all-male convention. Sarah listened carefully to her mother's end of the conversation. It sounded as though Dr. Calvin didn't even know about the boys-only rule.

Her mother handed the phone to Sarah. Dr. Calvin said she agreed the rule was wrong. She would gather the teachers before school on Monday morning and give them a choice: either they had to let girls in or, to be accurate to the period, they also had to keep out boys who weren't white. It would be up to each teacher. "Come see me second period on Monday," Dr. Calvin said.

When Sarah got to school on Monday, she went right to Mr. Star. She wanted to know which way he had decided. He seemed amused. Nothing had changed at all, he said.

"But didn't Dr. Calvin tell you?" Sarah asked.

His voice hardened. No changes, and that was final.

When the bell for second hour rang, Sarah went into the

from *It's Our World, Too!* by Phillip Hoose

Response notes

principal's office. Dr. Calvin closed the door. "Well?" she said. Sarah reported her conversation with Mr. Star.

Dr. Calvin frowned. Sarah looked at her, trying to decide whether to tell her that she was organizing a protest. It was an important decision. If Dr. Calvin approved, they could use the halls without fear of punishment, no matter what the teachers said. And it would be easier to talk her classmates into it if Sarah could assure them that they wouldn't get in trouble with the principal.

But if Dr. Calvin didn't approve, she would be watching for them and she would tell the teachers. There would be no way to surprise them then. And kids would be scared.

Sarah decided to risk it. Dr. Calvin was a woman, and she was black. Probably she had known discrimination in her own life. Even if she said no, Sarah was determined to protest anyway. There were only three days left to organize. She might as well find out what she was up against now.

"Dr. Calvin," Sarah said tentatively, "if Mr. Star isn't going to change his mind, some of us are planning to demonstrate in the halls during the convention."

Sarah thought there might have been a faint smile on the principal's lips. Dr. Calvin shrugged. "Well," she said, "then I guess you have to do what you have to do."

157

●◆ What are some words you might use to describe Sarah Rosen, her teacher, and her principal? Use the space below to make a "collage" of words that describe Sarah, Mr. Star, or Dr. Calvin. Before you begin, review the inferences you made while reading the selection.

●✦ What do you think happens at the girls' demonstration? Use your inferences to write a continuation of this article.

Inferences
help you read
"between the
lines."

Style and Structure

Have you ever watched a new house being built? Afterward, you may find that you view the finished house in a special way. When you know the depth of the foundation and the pattern of the framing, when you've watched how the doors were hung and the walls painted, your view of the house gains an added dimension.

In the same way, your view of literature gains an added dimension when you know about the craft of writing. An author creating a piece of literature is not so different from a carpenter building a house. Both choose materials, plan structures, and craft their work in their own unique styles.

As you begin to pay more attention to elements of language and craft in writing, you may find that you begin to view poems and stories in a whole new way.

Would you prefer a pet that *scuttles* or one that *bounds*? *Scuttle* and *bound* both mean "move quickly." But *scuttle* suggests the actions of an insect; *bound* suggests the actions of a much larger creature, such as a dog. So even though the question mentions neither animal directly, your answer will probably depend on your feelings about insects and dogs.

Authors often choose words that carry unspoken messages—words that help communicate feelings, moods, and attitudes. Your feelings about a selection may come, in part, from your responses to the author's choice of words. Noticing an author's word choice can help you understand more about the way a piece of writing affects you.

Read the poem below at least twice. Which words in it carry unspoken messages to you? Circle words that give you a positive or negative feeling, even if you're not sure why they do.

Response notes

160

let there be new flowering
Lucille Clifton

let there be new flowering
in the fields   let the fields
turn mellow for the men
let the men keep tender
through the time   let the time
be wrested from the war
let the war be won
let love be
at the end

Use a "feeling scale" to explore Clifton's word choices. Look at the words listed below, and find each one in the poem. Some may be words that you circled as you read. (If you're not sure of a word's meaning, look it up.) Write each listed word along the scale. Put each in the area that best shows how the word makes you feel.

flowering   fields   mellow   tender   time   wrested   war   love

strong
negative
feelings

mild
negative
feelings

neutral
feelings

mild
positive
feelings

strong
positive
feelings

●◆Lucille Clifton's poem is like a wish. In the space below, draw or write your own description of what the speaker in the poem wishes for.

●◆Add a note explaining how you feel about the wishes expressed in the poem.

Authors choose words carefully to create specific feelings in readers.

Some things that you read leave vivid pictures in your mind, long after you finish reading. These mental pictures are **images**, and authors create them with **sensory language**—words referring to things you can see, hear, touch, smell, or taste. Sensory images help you "put yourself there" as you read; they make poems and stories memorable.

May Swenson's "Waking from a Nap on the Beach" is filled with sensory images. As you read it, highlight each image that you notice. In the response notes, write which sense (or senses) the image appeals to. (The first one is done for you.)

Response notes

sense of sound

Waking from a Nap on the Beach
May Swenson

Sounds like big
rashers of bacon frying.
I look up from where I'm lying
expecting to see stripes

red and white. My eyes drop shut,
stunned by the sun.
Now the foam is flame, the long
troughs charcoal, but

still it chuckles and sizzles, it
burns and burns, it never gets done.
The sea is
fat.

● Which of the sensory images found in Swenson's poem creates the strongest impression of the beach for you? Explain your choice.

....

....

....

....

•◆Reread the poem. In your imagination, "put yourself there" with the speaker. Use the web below to focus on things about the beach that would appeal to each of your five senses. Complete each sentence starter with a descriptive phrase.

I taste...

I see...

Beach

I hear...

I smell...

I touch...

●◆ Use the phrases from your web on the previous page to create your own image poem.

Writers use sensory images to spark readers' imaginations and make literature memorable.

Three

A Thumbprint of Words

Word choice, language patterns, use of **imagery**—they are all part of an author's **style** (*how* an author writes, as opposed to *what* an author writes). Each author's style is as unique as a thumbprint. You may sometimes find yourself affected as much by an author's style as by the content of his or her writing. Noticing an author's style gives you another way to enjoy and understand your reading.

As you read the selection from *Maniac Magee,* look for the following elements of author Jerry Spinelli's style.

- He uses sentence fragments.
- He creates unusual comparisons (**similes** and **metaphors**).
- He chooses slang words and "sportswriter" terms.
- He builds vivid sensory images.

Try to underline at least one example of each element. In the response notes, mark *f* for fragments, *c* for comparisons, *s* for slang words and "sportswriter" terms, and *v* for vivid sensory images.

from *Maniac Magee* by Jerry Spinelli

Response notes

When Jeffrey Magee was next spotted, it was at the Little League field in the park. A Little League game had just ended. The Red Sox had won, but the big story was John McNab, who struck out sixteen batters to set a new Two Mills L. L. record.

McNab was a giant. He stood five feet eight and was said to weigh over a hundred and seventy pounds. He had to bring his birth certificate in to the League director to prove he was only twelve. And still most people didn't believe it.

The point is, the rest of the league was no match for McNab. It wouldn't have been so bad if he'd been a right-fielder, but he was a pitcher. And there was only one pitch he ever threw: a fastball.

Most of the batters never saw it; they just heard it whizzing past their noses. You could see their knees shaking from the stands. One poor kid stood there long enough to hear strike one go past, then threw up all over home plate.

It was still pretty light out, because when there are a lot of strikeouts, a game goes fast. And McNab was still on the mound, even though the official game was over. He figured he'd made baseball history, and he wanted to stretch it out as long as he could.

There were still about ten players around, Red Soxers and Green Soxers, and McNab was making them march up to the plate and take their swings. There was no catcher. The ball just zoomed to the backstop. When a kid struck out, he went back to the end of the line.

McNab was loving it. After each whiff, he laughed and bellowed the strikeout total. "Twenty-*six!* . . . Twenty-*seven!* . . . Twenty-*eight!* . . ." He was like a shark. He had the blood lust. The victims were hunched and trembling, walking the gangplank. "Thirty-*four!* . . . Thirty-*five!* . . ."

And then somebody new stepped up to the plate. Just a punky, runty little kid, no Red Sox or Green Sox uniform. Kind of scraggly. With a book, which he laid down on home plate. He scratched out a footing in the batter's box, cocked the bat on his shoulder, and stared at McNab.

McNab croaked from the mound, "Get outta there, runt. This is a Little League record. You ain't in Little League."

The kid walked away. Was he chickening out? No. He was lifting a red cap from the next batter in line. He put it on. He was back in the box.

McNab almost fell off the mound, he was laughing so hard. "Okay, runt. Number thirty-six coming up."

McNab fired. The kid swung. The batters in line automatically turned their eyes to the backstop, where the ball should be—but it wasn't there. It was in the air, riding on a beeline right out to McNab's head, the same line it came in on, only faster. McNab froze, then flinched, just in time. The ball missed his head but nipped the bill of his cap and sent it spinning like a flying saucer out to shortstop. The ball landed in the second-base dust and rolled all the way to the fence in center field.

Dead silence. Nobody moved.

McNab was gaping at the kid, who was still standing there all calm and cool, waiting for the next pitch. Finally a sort of grin slithered across McNab's lips. He roared: "Get my hat! Get the ball!"

Ten kids scrambled onto the field, bringing him the hat and ball. McNab had it figured now. He was so busy laughing at the runt, he lobbed him a lollipop and the runt got lucky and poled it.

This time McNab wasn't laughing. He fingered the ball, tips digging into the red stitching. He wound, he fired, he thought: *Man! That sucker's goin' so fast even I can hardly see it!* And then he was looking up, turning, following the flight of the ball, which finally came down to earth in deep left center field and bounced once to the fence.

More silence, except from someone who yelped "Yip—" then caught himself.

"Ball!" bellowed McNab.

He was handed the ball. He slammed his hat to the ground. His nostrils flared, he was breathing like a picadored bull. He

from *Maniac Magee* by Jerry Spinelli

Response notes

windmilled, reared, lunged, fired . . .

This time the ball cleared the fence on the fly.

No more holding back. The other kids cheered. Somebody ran for the ball. They were anxious now for more.

Three more pitches. Three more home runs.

Pandemonium on the sidelines. It was raining red and green hats.

McNab couldn't stand it. The next time he threw, it was right at the kid's head. The kid ducked. McNab called, "Strike one!"

Next pitch headed for the kid's belt. The kid bent his stomach around the ball. "Steee-rike *two!*"

Strike three took dead aim at the kid's knees, and here was the kid, swooping back and at the same time swatting at the ball like a golfer teeing off. It was the craziest baseball swing you ever saw, but there was the ball smoking out to center field.

●◆Write a note to a friend who is going to read *Maniac Magee* in class. From what you've read so far, describe Spinelli's style. Give your friend a couple of examples of what stands out for you.

167

◗ To see how style works, try rewriting the following passage from *Maniac Magee*. As you rewrite each line, change all sentence fragments into complete sentences, replace all slang terms with more formal words or phrases, and replace comparisons with new ones of your own.

"Ball!" bellowed McNab.

He was handed the ball. He slammed his hat to the ground. His nostrils flared, he was

breathing like a picadored bull. He windmilled, reared, lunged, fired . . .

This time the ball cleared the fence on the fly.

No more holding back. The other kids cheered. Somebody ran for the ball. They were

anxious now for more.

Three more pitches. Three more home runs.

Pandemonium on the sidelines. It was raining red and green hats.

In a small group, read one another's rewrites. Explore the effects of the changes in writing style. Share your observations with the class.

Every author has a unique way of using language. This is called the author's "style."

Four

Setting the Pace

As you read the selection from *Maniac Magee*, did you notice the tension building? Each time Maniac hits one of McNab's pitches, McNab gets a little angrier. You may have found yourself reading eagerly to see where the tension would lead.

Authors use sentence structure to help create the tension that keeps you reading. A longer, more detailed sentence can help to slow the action and build tension. A shorter sentence, with quick phrases, helps to speed the action and release tension.

Reread the excerpt from *Maniac Magee*. This time, in your response notes, jot *slow* where the story seems structured to move slowly and *fast* where the sentence structure seems to move more quickly.

●◆ Review the list of key events from *Maniac Magee* below. Then plot the events on the continuum to show the highs and lows of tension in the story.

1. McNab throws strikeout #26.

2. Maniac steps up to the plate.

3. Maniac hits McNab's first pitch.

4. McNab throws the ball at Maniac's head.

5. Maniac swings at the ball like a golfer teeing off.

169

①

← low tension → high tension

●◆ Look back at the sentence structure of the events you marked as high tension or low tension. How does the sentence structure affect the level of tension? Explain.

In the following passage from *Maniac Magee*, notice how Jerry Spinelli builds tension by using short sentences and sentence fragments:

> McNab was loving it. After each whiff, he laughed and bellowed the strikeout total. "Twenty-*six!* . . . Twenty-*seven!* . . . Twenty-*eight!* . . ." He was like a shark. He had the blood lust. The victims were hunched and trembling, walking the gangplank. "Thirty-*four!* . . . Thirty-*five!* . . ."

●◆Now try rewriting this passage using longer sentences and more detailed descriptions in order to slow the pace and bring the tension level *down*.

Sentence structure helps to set the pace of a story.

Five
Structure and Meaning

In poems, structure helps to show meaning. For instance, a new **stanza** usually signals a new idea or a new image. Poets also use structure for emphasis. To give a word or phrase special emphasis, the poet may place it at the end of a line or section or repeat a phrase or line. These techniques show readers which images, sounds, or ideas are important in the poem.

Some poems "shift" in the middle or near the end. A poet may create a shift by changing **tone**, by introducing a new image or idea, or by moving from the present to the past or future tense. If the poem has a message, the poet may state it after a shift.

As you read "The Courage That My Mother Had," circle repeated words and phrases. In the response notes, tell what you think the emphasis of the poem is.

Response notes

171

The Courage That My Mother Had
Edna St. Vincent Millay

The courage that my mother had
Went with her, and is with her still:
Rock from New England quarried;
Now granite in a granite hill.

The golden brooch my mother wore
She left behind for me to wear;
I have no thing I treasure more:
Yet, it is something I could spare.

Oh, if instead she'd left me
The thing she took into the grave!—
That courage like a rock, which she
Has no more need of, and I have.

●◆ Reread "The Courage That My Mother Had." After each stanza, close your eyes and reflect on the images—mental pictures—that come to mind. In the space below, draw one image for each stanza in the poem.

●◆ What do you consider the poem's main message? On your drawing, circle the part of the poem that makes this message clearest for you. Then state the message in your own words, or quote a part of the poem that seems to state it.

Poets use structure to show what ideas or images are important in a poem.

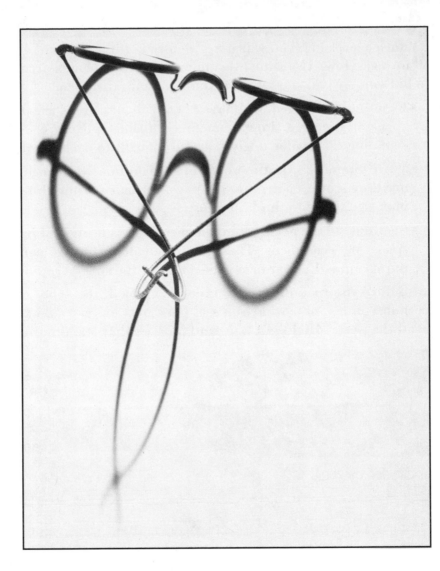

Active Reading: Poetry

When you read a poem, trust your own sense—including your sense of humor. Some poems are just for fun. All you have to do is relax and enjoy them. Other poems are like paintings, meant to convey images, perhaps in unusual ways. Still other poems tell stories or share emotions or insights.

No matter what type of poem you encounter, active reading strategies will help you get the most out of it. Poems are more compact than other kinds of writing. They may present images, emotions, and insights, but they don't always explain. So when you read poetry, it's up to you to make connections. Your eyes and your ears, your mind and your imagination all can help as you explore the craft of poetry.

Before exercising, you warm up. Before reading a poem, you need to warm up too. How? Use your eyes: notice how the poem is arranged on the page. What you see will start you on your way into the poem.

- **Framing** Does the poem have few words, leaving a great deal of white space on the page? Poets sometimes "frame" poems in white space, signaling the reader to give careful thought to each word.

- **Word Spacing** Are the words in straight lines with regular spacing, or are they scattered around the page? (Words scattered in unusual patterns may signal you to think in unusual patterns as you read.)

- **Sections** Is the poem all in one piece? Or is it divided into sections, with spaces between them? These sections, called **stanzas**, can work like paragraphs. Each stanza may show a different image, **viewpoint**, or idea.

Before you read the poem "Lineage," look at its layout on the page. In the response notes, note what you see. (One part has been done for you.) Then read the poem. **Highlight** lines and phrases that stand out as you read.

Response notes

word spacing: regular spaces, straight lines

Lineage
Margaret Walker

My grandmothers were strong.
They followed plows and bent to toil.
They moved through fields sowing seed.
They touched earth and grain grew.
They were full of sturdiness and singing.
My grandmothers were strong.

My grandmothers are full of memories
Smelling of soap and onions and wet clay
With veins rolling roughly over quick hands
They have many clean words to say.
My grandmothers were strong.
Why am I not as they?

174

●◆ Describe how Margaret Walker's poem looks on the page, paying special attention to framing, word spacing, and the poem's sections.

framing	word spacing	sections	other

●◆ What do you think Margaret Walker means by the question, "Why am I not as they?"

You can begin to understand a poem by looking at its layout on the page.

Two Tuning In

"What's going on here?"

That's a good question to ask about a poem. You can find out what's going on by paying attention to **sensory images**—mental pictures that appeal to the five senses. Think of poems as messages or images from poets. Some are like letters: they tell stories, express emotions, or share insights. Others are more like picture postcards: they are almost pure imagery.

When you read a poem, recreate the sensory images in your mind. As you reread, ask yourself what kind of message the poem represents. Is it more like a letter, or is it almost all imagery?

In "Finding a Lucky Number," pay attention to sensory images. Put question marks by parts that puzzle you; put exclamation points by parts that surprise you. Jot down questions and comments.

Response notes

176

Finding a Lucky Number
Gary Soto

When I was like you I crossed a street
To a store, and from the store
Up an alley, as I rolled chocolate
In my mouth and looked around
With my face. The day was blue
Between trees, even without wind,
And the fences were steaming
And a dog was staring into a paint bucket
And a Mexicano was raking
Spilled garbage into a box,
A raffle of eggshells and orange peels.
He nodded his head and I nodded mine
And rolled chocolate all the way
To the courthouse, where I sat
In the park, with a leaf falling
For every person who passed—
Three leaves and three daughters
With bags in their hands.
I followed them under trees,
The leaves rocking out of reach
Like those skirts I would love
From a distance. I lost them
When I bent down to tie my shoes
And begged a squirrel to eat grass.
Looking up, a dog on the run,
A grandma with a cart,
And Italians clicking dominoes
At a picnic table — men
Of the old world, in suits big enough
For Europe. I approached

Them like a squirrel, a tree
At a time, and when I was close
Enough to tell the hour from their wrists,
One laughed with hands in his hair
And turned to ask my age.
"Twelve," I said, and he knocked
My head softly with a knuckle:
"Lucky number, Sonny." He bared
His teeth, yellow and crooked
As dominoes, and tapped the front ones
With a finger. "I got twelve — see."
He opened wide until his eyes were lost
In the pouches of fat cheeks,
And I, not knowing what to do, looked in.

●◆ What do you think about this poem? Describe your responses.

....

....

....

●◆ After you've read the poem several times, close your eyes. Visualize one
clear image that the poem has left in your mind. Next, open your eyes and
sketch the image. Then add notes explaining your sketch.

Poets
use sensory images to
help convey their messages
and create strong
impressions.

Three
Beyond Words

In one famous poem, Carl Sandburg describes fog that comes in "on little cat feet." Sandburg's figure of speech, comparing fog to a cat, suggests much more than it says. By exploring **figures of speech**—similes, metaphors, and personification—you can deepen your understanding of a poem. To explore Sandburg's figure of speech, you might use the following steps:

1. **Question** Ask yourself, "How is fog like a cat?"

2. **Picture** In your mind, picture both fog and a cat. You might notice that both move silently and look soft. You might feel that both can be beautiful, mysterious, or even menacing.

3. **Reflect** Think about your responses. You might decide that the figure of speech suggests that fog is soft and mysterious. (You could check your interpretation by reading the rest of the poem.)

Read Mary TallMountain's "There Is No Word for Goodbye." Then read it again, pausing at each figure of speech you find. Use the three steps above to explore each figure of speech. Jot or sketch your responses in the response notes.

Response notes

There Is No Word for Goodbye
Mary TallMountain

Sokoya, I said, looking through
    the net of wrinkles into
    wise black pools
    of her eyes.

What do you say in Athabaskan
    when you leave each other?
    What is the word
    for goodbye?

A shade of feeling rippled
    the wind-tanned skin.
    Ah, nothing, she said,
    watching the river flash.

She looked at me close.
    We just say, Tlaa. That means,
    See you.
    We never leave each other.
    When does your mouth
    say goodbye to your heart?

She touched me light
    as a bluebell.
    You forget when you leave us,
    You're so small then.
    We don't use that word.

We always think you're coming back,
    but if you don't,
    we'll see you some place else.
    You understand.
    There is no word for goodbye.

Response notes

➛ Which parts of the poem are most vivid for you? Explain.

179

Four figures of speech from "There Is No Word for Goodbye" are listed below. Choose one of them as a springboard for a short poem of your own.

- ". . . looking through / the net of wrinkles . . ."
- "wise black pools / of her eyes . . ."
- "When does your mouth / say goodbye to your heart?"
- "She touched me light / as a bluebell."

✒ In your poem, use images that came to you as you explored the figure of speech in Mary TallMountain's poem. Read over your response notes for ideas. Then, in the space below, brainstorm a list of images that you might use.

✒ Choose images from your brainstorming list as a starting point for your poem. Add additional figures of speech and details to make your poem vivid. Write your poem in the space below.

Exploring figures of speech deepens your insights into a poem.

Four
Word Music

Poetry is written to be seen *and* heard, so be sure to read poetry aloud. Listen for **rhymes** at the ends of lines, and listen for "echoes" within the poem. The poem may include several words with the same consonant sounds (**consonance**). Or it may include several words with the same vowel sounds (**assonance**). Notice how those sounds echo. For example, in "Adventures of Isabel," below, look at line 4. The / b / sounds in *bear's* and *big* echo each other, as do the / k / sounds in *cruel* and *cavernous*. In lines 9 and 11, the / ā / sounds in *straightened* and *ate* echo each other. Poets use sounds for emphasis or to enhance the **rhythm** of the poem,

Read "Adventures of Isabel" silently and then read it aloud. Underline rhymes with one colored marker and echoes (consonance and assonance) with another.

Adventures of Isabel
Ogden Nash

Isabel met an enormous bear,
Isabel, Isabel, didn't care;
The bear was hungry, the bear was ravenous,
The bear's big mouth was cruel and cavernous.
The bear said, Isabel, glad to meet you,
How do, Isabel, now I'll eat you!
Isabel, Isabel, didn't worry,
Isabel didn't scream or scurry,
She washed her hands and she straightened her
    hair up,
Then Isabel quietly ate the bear up.

Once in a night as black as pitch
Isabel met a wicked witch.
The witch's face was cross and wrinkled,
The witch's gums with teeth were sprinkled.
Ho, ho, Isabel! the old witch crowed,
I'll turn you into an ugly toad!
Isabel, Isabel, didn't worry,
Isabel didn't scream or scurry,
She showed no rage, she showed no rancor,
But she turned the witch into milk and drank her.

Response notes

181

Response notes

ADVENTURES OF ISABEL (continued)

Isabel met a hideous giant,
Isabel continued self-reliant.
The giant was hairy, the giant was horrid,
He had one eye in the middle of his forehead.
Good morning, Isabel, the giant said,
I'll grind your bones to make my bread.
Isabel, Isabel, didn't worry,
Isabel didn't scream or scurry.
She nibbled the zwieback that she always fed off,
And when it was gone, she cut the giant's head off.

Isabel met a troublesome doctor,
He punched and he poked till he really shocked her.
The doctor's talk was of coughs and chills
And the doctor's satchel bulged with pills.
The doctor said unto Isabel,
Swallow this, it will make you well.
Isabel, Isabel, didn't worry,
Isabel didn't scream or scurry.
She took those pills from the pill concoctor,
And Isabel calmly cured the doctor.

182

●◆Ogden Nash is famous for his playful use of rhymes and echoes. Which parts of this poem do you find most humorous? How do the rhymes and echoes add to the humor? Explain your response.

●◆ To understand the role of rhymes in this poem, see what it's like without them. Look back over the poem and find three or four rhyming words that you could replace with synonyms that don't rhyme. (For example, you could replace *ravenous* with *hungry* or *cavernous* with *large*.) Now insert the new words above or next to the original words. Reread the poem. How is the effect of your new poem different from the original?

....

....

....

....

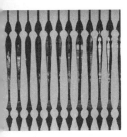

●◆ Now try creating some rhymes. Add at least two lines of your own to the poem about Isabel. Make your lines rhyme and use some words that echo. **183**

....

....

....

....

....

....

....

....

Noticing rhymes and echoes helps you hear the music of a poem.

Five
The Beat Goes On

If you've ever listened to rap, you know that language has a beat, just as music does. When you read a poem aloud, listen for its **rhythm**, or **meter**. A poem's meter may be regular and predictable, or it may vary. Even an unrhymed poem may have meter.

Repetition makes another kind of rhythm. Poets may repeat key words or phrases for emphasis. Or they may repeat language patterns, expressing similar kinds of ideas in similar ways. Meter and repetition help to create the **mood**—the emotional feel—of a poem.

In "Life Doesn't Frighten Me," poet Maya Angelou uses varied, jazzy rhythms. Read the poem silently; then read it aloud. Listen for patterns of meter and repetition and notice when the patterns change. Mark changes with a star in your response notes.

Response notes

Life Doesn't Frighten Me
Maya Angelou

Shadows on the wall
Noises down the hall
Life doesn't frighten me at all
Bad dogs barking loud
Big ghosts in a cloud
Life doesn't frighten me at all.

Mean old Mother Goose
Lions on the loose
They don't frighten me at all
Dragons breathing flame
On my counterpane
That doesn't frighten me at all.

I go boo
Make them shoo
I make fun
Way they run
I won't cry
So they fly
I just smile
They go wild
Life doesn't frighten me at all.

184

Tough guys in a fight
All alone at night
Life doesn't frighten me at all.
Panthers in the park
Strangers in the dark
No, they don't frighten me at all.

That new classroom where
Boys all pull my hair
(Kissy little girls
With their hair in curls)
They don't frighten me at all.

Don't show me frogs or snakes
And listen for my scream,
If I'm afraid at all
It's only in my dreams.

I've got a magic charm
That I keep up my sleeve,
I can walk the ocean floor
And never have to breathe.

Life doesn't frighten me at all
Not at all.
Not at all.
Life doesn't frighten me at all.

185

●◆ How does the rhythm of this poem make you feel? Explain your response.

....

....

....

....

....

....

....

With a small group of classmates, tap out the rhythms of the poem. (Don't be surprised if group members' ideas of the rhythms vary. Keep working until your group reaches consensus.) Then plan and present your version of the poem. Decide whether your group will read the entire poem together, or whether some stanzas will be solos. Plan which lines will be louder and which will be softer. You might add motions or dance steps. Make your version show the feelings that the poem gives you. Practice the poem as a group, and then present it to your class.

●◆In the space below, compare the various versions of the poem the class presented. How did different groups achieve different effects? Which presentation of the poem appealed to you most? Why?

Rhythms in poetry help to communicate feelings to readers.

Active Reading: Persuasive Writing

What is persuasion? When someone is trying to persuade you, he or she wants to get you to see things from a certain viewpoint or perspective. Advertisements, movie previews, political speeches, and book reviews are all forms of persuasion. In each case, the "persuader" wants you to agree with his or her opinions or to take certain actions (for example, to go see a new movie).

Writers use many strategies to persuade readers to agree with their opinions. They choose words that make the reader feel emotional about a subject; they use facts and details to support their opinions; they write in a tone that gets their message across; and they "slant" their writing to favor their argument. Learning to recognize these strategies can help you decide whether you are persuaded by the writer's ideas—or just the writer's persuasive techniques.

Would you rather wear something that is *inexpensive* or *cheap*? Would you rather be described as *young* or *childish*? These words make you feel differently because they have different connotations. A **denotation** is a word's "dictionary meaning." A **connotation** is the emotional meaning in addition to its dictionary meaning. The denotations of *cottage* and *shack*, for example, are close to being the same: both are places to live. But one word (*cottage*) has a positive emotional meaning, while the other (*shack*) has a negative one. When you come across words with strong connotations, be careful. You need to separate your emotions from the facts when you are deciding whether to accept a writer's opinions.

The following article, "Hearing the Sweetest Songs," is written by Nicolette Toussaint, who is hearing impaired. Before you read, think about the word *disabled*. What is the denotation of the word? (Use a dictionary if you need help.) What are some of the connotations people have of the word *disabled*? Jot down your ideas in the chart below.

DISABLED

Denotation:

Connotations:

As you read the article, put a plus (+) in the response notes next to any words or phrases that give a positive connotation of *disabled* or *hearing impaired*. Put a minus (–) near words that give a negative connotation.

"Hearing the Sweetest Songs" by Nicolette Toussaint

Every year when I was a child, a man brought a big, black, squeaking machine to school. When he discovered I couldn't hear all his peeps and squeaks, he would get very excited. The nurse would draw a chart with a deep canyon in it. Then I would listen to the squeaks two or three times, while the adults—who were all acting very, very nice—would watch me raise my hand. Sometimes I couldn't tell whether I heard the squeaks or just imagined them, but I liked being the center of attention.

My parents said I lost my hearing to pneumonia as a baby, but I knew I hadn't *lost* anything. None of my parts had dropped off. Nothing had changed: if I wanted to listen to Beethoven, I could put my head between the speakers and turn the dial up to 7. I could hear jets at the airport a block away. I could hear my mom when she was in the same room—if I wanted to. I could even hear my cat purr if I put my good ear right on top of him.

I wasn't aware of *not* hearing until I began to wear a hearing aid at the age of 30. It shattered my peace: shoes creaking, papers crackling, pencils tapping, phones ringing, refrigerators humming, people cracking knuckles, clearing throats and blowing noses! Cars, bikes, dogs, cats, kids all seemed to appear from nowhere and fly right at me.

I was constantly startled, unnerved, agitated—exhausted. I felt as though inquisitorial Nazis in an old World War II film were burning the side of my head with a merciless white spotlight. Under that onslaught, I had to break down and confess: I couldn't hear. Suddenly, I began to discover many things I couldn't do.

I couldn't identify sounds. One afternoon, while lying on my side watching a football game on TV, I kept hearing a noise that sounded like my cat playing with a flexible-spring doorstop. I checked, but the cat was asleep. Finally, I happened to lift my head as the noise occurred. Heard through my good ear, the metallic buzz turned out to be the referee's whistle.

I couldn't tell where sounds came from. I couldn't find my phone under the blizzard of papers on my desk. The more it rang, the deeper I dug. I shoveled mounds of paper onto the floor and finally had to track it down by following the cord from the wall.

When I lived alone, I felt helpless because I couldn't hear alarm clocks, vulnerable because I couldn't hear the front door open and frightened because I wouldn't hear a burglar until it was too late.

●◆ What do you think about what the author has to say?

●◆ Look back to where you marked your pluses and minuses in the response notes. What are some of the positive and negative connotations of *disabled* or *hearing impaired* that appear in Toussaint's article? Are the connotations mostly positive or negative? What does this tell you about how the author wants you to feel about her topic?

Now try using connotations and denotations to persuade. Write two menus for your school lunch. Menu One should use denotations—write exactly what is being served. Menu Two should use connotations. Use words to make students feel better about what they get to eat . . . or use words that reveal the ugly truth!

1.

Today's Menu

(Denotations)

191

2.

Today's Menu

(Connotations)

Writers use connotations to encourage their readers to respond emotionally to a topic.

Why do you write? Do you make lists to keep track of things? Do you record thoughts in a **journal**? Do you write stories or letters? Like you, professional authors write for different reasons, or purposes. Newspaper reporters write to inform you of events. Novelists write stories to entertain readers. Travel writers describe faraway places. And other writers write to persuade, to try to change the reader's perspective.

As you read the rest of "Hearing the Sweetest Songs," try to figure out Toussaint's perspective on this topic. Where is the writer coming from? What does she want you to think? Jot down your impressions in the response notes as you read.

← Response notes

"Hearing the Sweetest Songs" (continued)
by Nicolette Toussaint

Then one day I missed a job interview because of the phone. I had gotten off the subway twenty minutes early, eager and dressed to the nines. But the address I had written down didn't exist! I must have misheard it. I searched the street, becoming overheated, late and frantic, knowing that if I confessed that I couldn't hear on the phone, I would make my odds of getting hired even worse.

For the first time, I felt unequal, disadvantaged, and disabled. Now that I had something to compare, I knew that I had lost something; not just my hearing, but my independence and my sense of wholeness. I had always hated to be seen as inferior, so I never mentioned my lack of hearing. Unlike a wheelchair or a white cane, my disability doesn't announce itself. For most of my life, I chose to pass as abled, and I thought I did it quite well.

But after I got the hearing aid, a business friend said, "You know, Nicolette, you think you get away with not hearing, but you don't. Sometimes in meetings you answer the wrong question. People don't know you can't hear, so they think you're daydreaming, eccentric, stupid—or just plain rude. It would be better to just tell them."

I wondered about that then, and I still do. If I tell, I risk being seen as *unable* rather than *disabled*. Sometimes, when I say I can't hear, the waiter will turn to my companion and say, "What does she want?" as though I have lost my power of speech.

If I tell, people may see *only* my disability. Once someone is labeled "deaf," "crippled," "mute" or "aged," that's too often all they are. I'm a writer, a painter, a slapdash housekeeper, a gardener who grows wondrous roses; my hearing is just part of the whole. It's a tender part, and you should handle it with

"Hearing the Sweetest Songs" (continued)
by Nicolette Toussaint

Response notes

care. But like most people with a disability, I don't mind if you ask about it.

In fact, you should ask, because it's an important part of me, something my friends see as part of my character. My friend Anne always rests a hand on my elbow in parking lots, since several times, drivers who assume that I hear them have nearly run me over. When I hold my head at a certain angle, my husband, Mason, will say "It's a plane" or "It's a siren." And my mother loves to laugh about the things I *thought* I heard: last week I was told that "the Minotaurs in the garden are getting out of hand." I imagined capering bullmen and I was disappointed to learn that all we had in the garden were overgrown "baby tears."

Not hearing can be funny, or frustrating. And once in a while, it can be the cause of something truly transcendent. One morning at the shore I was listening to the ocean when Mason said, "Hear the bird?" What bird? I listened hard until I heard a faint, unbirdlike, croaking sound. If he hadn't mentioned it, I would never have noticed it. As I listened, slowly I began to hear—or perhaps imagine—a distant song. Did I *really* hear it? Or just hear in my heart what he shared with me? I don't care. Songs imagined are as sweet as songs heard, and songs shared are sweeter still.

That sharing is what I want for all of us. We're all just temporarily abled, and every one of us, if we live long enough, will become disabled in some way. Those of us who have gotten there first can tell you how to cope with phones and alarm clocks. About ways of holding a book, opening a door and leaning on a crutch all at the same time. And what it's like to give up in despair on Thursday, then begin all over again on Friday, because there's no other choice—and because the roses are beginning to bud in the garden.

These are conversations we all should have, and it's not that hard to begin. Just let me see your lips when you speak. Stay in the same room. Don't shout. And ask what you want to know.

●❖Look back at your notes. What is Nicolette Toussaint's viewpoint? What is she trying to persuade you to think or to do? Create a web on the next page. Write Toussaint's viewpoint in the middle. On the arms of the web, write the important points she makes to support her view.

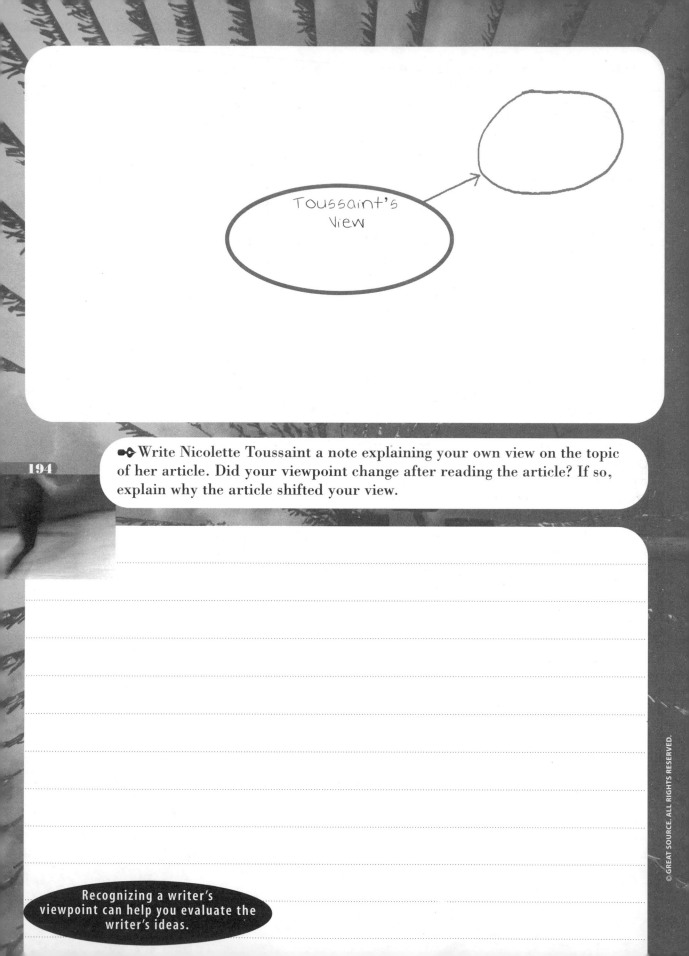

Toussaint's
View

●◆ Write Nicolette Toussaint a note explaining your own view on the topic
of her article. Did your viewpoint change after reading the article? If so,
explain why the article shifted your view.

194

Recognizing a writer's
viewpoint can help you evaluate the
writer's ideas.

Three
Taking Sides

Imagine that when you came to school today, everyone whose name starts with the letter *L* was treated differently. The *L*s were allowed to pick their own seats and talk during class. They were the first to be dismissed for lunch. And, when they got to the cafeteria, they were served pepperoni pizza while everyone else got just a slice of bread. What would you call this kind of treatment? Unless your name starts with *L*, you'd probably call it unfair! It's also called biased.

Bias is strongly favoring someone or something. Some writing is unbiased. There are no "sides," for example, in a news article about a storm. But all persuasive writing does have bias—some idea or person is favored over another.

As you read "The Myth of the Computer," try to figure out the writer's bias. First, you'll need to decide what issue the writer is addressing. Then you can decide what the writer's bias is, or what "side" he is taking.

"The Myth of the Computer" by Steven Levy

Response notes

I was 30 years old before I touched a computer, and, to be honest, until that point I felt I hadn't missed much. After all, in 1981 computers were still known to most of us as big, ugly objects that did something *to* you, not friendly little desktop devices that allowed you to do something. There was the idea that computers could be used in education, but only as mental drill instructors, demanding right answers without a smile. Now, of course, we all believe that the machines are destined to be full partners in the learning process, and woe betide the middle-class parent who doesn't provide computer access to little Travis or Felicity.

My own career is intimately entwined with the digital revolution. So prepare for a heresy: I'm not sure how good computers really are for kids.

My own progeny, born in 1990, was perched before a screen well before he turned 2, with more familiarity with a wired mouse than the squeaky variety. He took for granted what 20 years ago would have been considered outrageous: unlimited access to a computing machine with more power than the room-filling multi-million-dollar military behemoths of the past. But what did he do with it? At its best, he learned some problem-solving by figuring out the proper order that Putt-Putt the automobile should tackle his chores. He recognized more words by blasting them out of the sky before they hit the ground. He had stories read to him, accompanied by animated illustrations. He toyed with maps, he painted pictures, he double-clicked on dinosaur parts, he built houses with virtual Legos, he sailed a pirate ship. That, as I said, was the best of it.

There is the worst of it, too. He spends a lot of time with silly and sometimes overly aggressive programs. His earliest instinct was to avoid software with the highest claims of cognitive nutrition. Whenever I presented him with a new package, his first question would be "Is this a winning game?" because he came to learn that the ones that kept score provided more kicks.

And though I was happy that he had learned so-called computer literacy, it was clear that in and of itself, this was no boon. My wife and I quickly came to understand that while the computer can be just as effective a babysitter as the television is, leaving your kid alone with a computer for hours isn't necessarily better than Saturday-morning cartoons. (Especially when he winds up seeing the same characters on both screens.)

In short, I'm happier to see the kid with a book.

I fully expect that as my son grows, the computer will become as inseparable from his work as it is with mine. When he complains about having to perfect his penmanship, I secretly agree with him—the days of scriveners are gone, and he won't need it. By the time he hits high school, I expect that all his writings will be word-processed, and I will be severely disappointed if the marketplace doesn't provide schools with very low-cost computers so that all students can partake of these tools, at their desks and out of school as well. I anticipate that homework will be transformed dramatically by the resources on the Internet—as well as the ability to network with fellow classmates and even the teacher.

Do these sound like the same sorts of tasks performed by computer users in the professional world? Sure do. In the years since computers have been commonly available, we've found out what they're good for. It won't be surprising to find out that in the education world, they're good for the same things. So maybe it would be helpful to more carefully examine the myths and misrepresentations about what we *want* computers to do for our kids. We know that they can be entertaining. And it's great that they provide a means to augment learning, sometimes through startlingly creative programs. But as for computers being a learning panacea, forget it. The superstar of education is still the book.

The line below is called a continuum. The middle of the line is "neutral," while each end of the line is an "extreme." Above the line, write a word or two that states the topic of the article. At each end of the continuum, write an "extreme" opinion about the topic—the two ends should be opposite. (One end could be something like "Computers are the best learning tools for kids.")

TOPIC:

Extreme Opinion (positive) — Neutral — Extreme Opinion (negative)

Now that your continuum is ready, mark an "X" on the line to show the writer's bias. Share your placement with others in a small group. Explain your response. Be sure to use specific examples from the article that point out the bias.

Where do you stand on this topic? Jot down your thoughts on the article. Then mark a "Y" on the line to show your bias.

Biased writing tries to persuade the reader to see an issue from one particular side.

Four

Separating Fact from Opinion

A **fact** is something that can be proven to be true or false. An **opinion**, on the other hand, is someone's personal idea or feeling about something. Opinions cannot be proven true or false. Usually, persuasive writing includes both facts and opinions. The goal of persuasion is to convince readers to adopt an opinion. Sometimes, the best way to convince people of an opinion is by giving them facts. When a friend has told you something that doesn't sound believable, have you ever said "Prove it!"? That's the task of a persuasive writer—to "prove it."

Reread "The Myth of the Computer." Circle facts and underline opinions. In the response notes, jot down any ideas you have about the way that Steven Levy proves his point.

●◆ What is Steven Levy's view of computers?

●◆ Now evaluate Levy's argument. Does he try to persuade mostly with facts or mostly opinions? Write down at least two of his facts and two opinions. How well do you think he proves his point? Explain.

●◆Imagine you are asked to debate this topic. Choose your "side." Then write some notes to use during the debate. Include both opinions and facts to support your viewpoint.

My viewpoint:

Opinions:

199

facts that support my opinions:

Writers
use facts to support their
viewpoints.

Read the following scenarios:

Scenario 1:

You have been struggling with your pitching for weeks. At a summer baseball clinic, a major-league player teaches you a few of his tricks for getting the ball over the plate. When he's finished, you say, "Thanks a lot for your help!"

Scenario 2:

You and your younger brother are supposed to clean the kitchen after dinner—together. While you clear the table, he plays a video game. While you wash and dry the dishes, he talks on the phone. When you leave the kitchen, you say, "Thanks a lot for your help!"

In each of the situations above, how would you say the words "Thanks a lot for your help!"? Say them out loud with a partner. The way you said these words was your **tone**. (A speaker's or writer's tone expresses the person's attitude about a topic.) In the first case, your tone was probably sincere and excited, while in the second, your tone was probably sarcastic.

Persuasive writers use tone, too. For serious topics, a writer might choose a tone that is solemn or thoughtful. For an advertisement or a campaign brochure, a writer might choose a tone that is exciting or positive. As you read the excerpt from *All I Really Need to Know I Learned in Kindergarten*, think about what kind of tone Robert Fulghum uses. Write words that describe the tone in the response notes as you read.

← Response notes →

from *All I Really Need to Know I Learned in Kindergarten*
by Robert Fulghum

All I really need to know about how to live and what to do and how to be I learned in kindergarten. Wisdom was not at the top of the graduate-school mountain, but there in the sandpile at Sunday School. These are the things I learned:
Share everything.
Play fair.
Don't hit people.
Put things back where you found them.
Clean up your own mess.
Don't take things that aren't yours.
Say you're sorry when you hurt somebody.
Wash your hands before you eat.
Flush.
Warm cookies and cold milk are good for you.
Live a balanced life—learn some and think some and draw and paint and sing and dance and play and work every day some.

from *All I Really Need to Know I Learned in Kindergarten*
by Robert Fulghum

Take a nap every afternoon.

When you go out into the world, watch out for traffic, hold hands, and stick together.

Be aware of wonder. Remember the little seed in the Styrofoam cup: The roots go down and the plant goes up and nobody really knows how or why, but we are all like that.

Goldfish and hamsters and white mice and even the little seed in the Styrofoam cup—they all die. So do we.

And then remember the Dick-and-Jane books and the first word you learned—the biggest word of all—LOOK.

Everything you need to know is in there somewhere. The Golden Rule and love and basic sanitation. Ecology and politics and equality and sane living.

Take any one of those items and extrapolate it into sophisticated adult terms and apply it to your family life or your work or your government or your world and it holds true and clear and firm. Think what a better world it would be if we all—the whole world—had cookies and milk about three o'clock every afternoon and then lay down with our blankies for a nap. Or if all governments had as a basic policy to always put things back where they found them and to clean up their own mess.

And it is still true, no matter how old you are—when you go out into the world, it is best to hold hands and stick together.

●◆ First, think about the opinion that Fulghum expresses in his essay. Sum up his opinion. Imagine that this excerpt is a newspaper article, and write a headline for it.

Daily News

●❖How would you describe the tone of the excerpt? Draw an image that represents the tone. (For example, if you'd describe Fulghum's tone as angry, you might draw an "angry face.")

●❖Do you think his tone helps Fulghum persuade readers? Why or why not?

....

....

....

....

....

....

....

....

Persuasive writers use tone to encourage their readers to feel a certain way about a topic.

Focus on the Writer: Gary Paulsen

Some writers explore one idea or theme in many different works. In several of his novels, writer Gary Paulsen explores the theme of *challenge*.

Paulsen's own life has held a variety of challenges. He moved frequently from place to place with his military family and took on many jobs to help support himself when he was young. As an adult, Paulsen landed a plane in an emergency, battled an angry moose, and took dangerous spills during the Iditarod sled race.

Many of Paulsen's characters face challenges, too. As you read Paulsen's stories, think about the challenges the characters face and how they are changed as a result.

One An Author's Style

Riding on a sled down a snowy mountain behind a pack of dogs . . . surviving on your own in the wilderness . . . facing an angry bear close up. As Gary Paulsen explores these situations in his books, he uses language and a writing **style** that help the reader feel the excitement, the intensity— and sometimes the danger—of a challenge.

In Paulsen's novel *Hatchet*, Brian Robeson survives alone in the wilderness for fifty-four days with nothing but a hatchet. In *The River*, Paulsen continues Brian's story. This time, Brian goes back into the wilderness with Derek Holtzer, a psychologist who wants to learn about Brian's survival techniques. As you read the excerpt from *The River*, pay attention to how Paulsen writes and the words he uses. In the response notes, jot down how Paulsen's writing makes you feel.

response notes

204

from ***The River*** by Gary Paulsen

He rolled on his side. His body felt stiff, mashed into the ground, and the sudden movement made his vision blur.

There.

He saw Derek—or the form of Derek. He was facedown on his bed, his right hand out, his left arm back and down his side. Blurred, he was all blurred and asleep—how could he be all blurred? Brian shook his head, tried to focus.

Derek was still asleep. How strange, Brian thought—how strange that Derek should still be asleep in the bright daylight, and he knew then that Derek was not sleeping, but did not want to think of the other thing.

Let's reason it out, he thought, his mind as blurred as his vision. Reason it all out. Derek was reaching for the radio and briefcase and the lightning hit the tree next to the shelter and came down the tree and across the air and into Derek and he fell . . .

No.

He was still asleep.

He wasn't that other thing. Not that other word.

But Brian's eyes began to clear then and he saw that Derek was lying with his head to the side and that it was facing Brian and the eyes weren't closed.

They were open.

He was on his side not moving and his eyes were open and Brian thought how strange it was that he would sleep that way—mashed on his stomach.

He knew Derek wasn't sleeping.

He knew.

"No. . . ."

from *The River* by Gary Paulsen

He couldn't be. Couldn't be . . . dead. Not Derek.

Finally, he accepted it.

Brian rose to his hands and knees, stiff and with great slowness, and crawled across the floor of the shelter to where Derek lay.

The large man lay on his stomach as he'd dropped, his head turned to the left. The eyes were not fully open, but partially lidded, and the pupils stared blankly, unfocused toward the back of the shelter.

Brian touched his cheek. He remembered how when the pilot had his heart attack he had felt cool—the dead skin had felt cool.

Derek's skin did not have the coolness, it felt warm; and Brian kneeled next to him and saw that he was breathing.

Tiny little breaths, his chest barely rising and falling, but he was breathing, the air going in and out, and he was not the other word—not dead—and Brian leaned over him.

"Derek?"

There was no answer, no indication that Derek had heard him.

"Derek. Can you hear anything I'm saying?"

Still no sign, no movement.

205

●◆ Look back at the notes you took while you read. How do Paulsen's words and writing style make you feel about Brian and the challenge he faces?

Look at how short many of Paulsen's sentences and paragraphs are. Listen as you take turns reading the passage aloud with a partner. Paulsen's writing has been called staccato—it happens in short but loud "bursts."

●◆ Now try using Paulsen's "staccato" style. Continue Paulsen's story from this point. Write a few paragraphs using words and sentences that continue the tension and excitement. Some sentences should be short: only 4–6 words long.

206

A writer's style can affect the impressions readers get as they read.

Two Real-Life Characters

In Paulsen's *Dancing Carl*, the character of Carl is based on Paulsen's own father. Paulsen's father came home from World War II with both physical and mental scars. In the story, Carl returns many years after the war to the small town where he grew up.

In this excerpt, Marsh (the narrator) and his friend Willy are down at the local ice rink. They know that Carl returned from the war with "troubles" and that the town council helped him by giving him a job at the rink and lodging in the warming house. In the warming house, as they get ready to play hockey, Marsh and Willy learn something new about Carl. As you read the excerpt from *Dancing Carl*, jot down your ideas about what Carl is like in the response notes.

from *Dancing Carl* by Gary Paulsen

Response notes

No matter how much you do in the summer, no matter how hard you work or run, your ankles always get weak. The muscles you use for skating don't get used in the summer and it's like everybody has to start all over in the fall, or the first part of winter when the ice forms and gets tight.

The next day was a Friday. School was school. But everybody brought skates and after school we hit the rinks and it was cold and dusky and we went into the warming house to put our skates on.

It was packed. It usually is the first few times after the ice is formed. But this time for some reason there were a lot of little kids, three and four, and like always they were having a rough time.

After skating gets going the warming house isn't so crowded. People skate and come in for a little, then back out, and cycle through that way. But when it first opens they just pack in and the little kids get pushed sideways until they're all in one corner, standing holding their skates, pouting and some of them starting to cry and always before they just had to fight it out or wait until the bigger kids were done and out skating.

But now there was Carl.

He was in the back of the shack and he stood up and he moved into the middle and he took a little girl by the hand and shouldered people out of the way and moved to the benches by the door. There were other kids sitting there, high-school kids suiting up for hockey and he looked at them.

That's all he did. Just looked at them, standing up with his flight jacket unzipped and the little girl holding onto his hand and Willy and I were sitting where we could see his eyes.

207

from ***Dancing Carl*** by Gary Paulsen

"They look hot," he said to me, leaning close to my ear. "His eyes look hot."

And they did. They almost glowed when he looked down at the kids who were sitting on the bench.

For a second or two they didn't do anything, and I think maybe they didn't want to do anything either. But the eyes cut through them, and they moved sideways and some of them got up and they left a place for the little girl and still Carl stood, looking down.

They moved more, made a wider place, and then the people in the center of the room parted and Carl raised his hand and the children who had been pushed down and down came through and they started to use the bench by the door and from that time on whenever the little kids came in they used that part of the bench and nobody else would use that place. Not even the grownups who came to skate to the music.

What does Marsh learn when Carl helps the little girl in the warming house? Brainstorm a list of character traits—words that describe what you know about Carl based on this scene.

●◗ Think of someone you know who would make an interesting character in a story. Fill out the character sketch chart.

The "real" person: ....

Name of Character: ....

Traits/Experiences I can use in the story	Things I plan to add or change

Basing a character on a real person helps writers create characters that seem vivid and real.

Three
Personal Challenges

Characters are often faced with obstacles or challenges. Personal or emotional challenges can cause characters to change in important ways. As you read about characters who confront personal or emotional challenges, think about how these experiences change them.

In this passage from *Dancing Carl*, Marsh brings a model of a B-17 to the rink to show Carl. It is through Carl's reaction to the model that Marsh and Willy begin to understand the emotional scars that Carl still carries as the result of the war. As you read the excerpt, jot down ideas about why Carl reacts as he does—and why the model affects him so strongly.

Response notes

from ***Dancing Carl*** by Gary Paulsen

Somehow we got to the rinks, either with the B-17 flying and carrying me along or with me holding it down, and there wasn't anybody skating.

Not even any kids. So we went in the warming house half figuring it would be closed but Carl was sitting on his bunk.

He smiled when we came in, then his face tightened in a quick frown when he saw the plane but I didn't think anything of it.

We knocked snow off and I put the skates and stick in a corner. There was nobody else in the warming house either.

"What's that?" he said, pointing at the stick model.

"It's a model I made. It's a B-17."

"I know that. I know what it is. I mean why do you have it here at the rink?"

"I told him he was crazy . . ." Willy started, laughing.

"Get it out of here."

His voice was quiet, almost like a still pond. Not mad sounding or sad, maybe a little afraid, but so quiet and still that I couldn't quite hear it.

"What?"

"Please take it outside. The model. Please take it out now."

"But it's just a model. If I take it out the wind will tear it apart." Like I said, I had a lot of work in it. I'd probably ruin it later, the way you do with models. Maybe put lighter fluid on the tail and send her off a roof. But that was later, now it was still a fresh model and I hated to just throw it out in the snow and let the wind tear it apart. "I'll put it over in the corner."

"Did you have something to do with B-17's during the war?" Willy asked and it was something he shouldn't have asked, not then, not ever.

© GREAT SOURCE. ALL RIGHTS RESERVED.

from *Dancing Carl* by Gary Paulsen

Carl turned from the plane to Willy and there was a hunted look in his eyes. No, more than that, more a torn thing, a broken thing—as if something inside had ripped and torn loose and left him broken and he looked at the model and his face wrinkled down and I knew it wasn't a model anymore, knew he wasn't in the warming house.

"Colors," he said, whispering. "Colors red and down and going around and around in tighter and tighter circles. Hot. Colors hot and alive and going down."

Willy stepped back. "I'm sorry. I didn't mean to say anything . . ."

But it was done. His whisper changed to a hiss, hot and alive, and he stood in the warming house and got into the open place by the door. I dumped the model in a corner, dumped it without looking, and moved away.

Carl stood with his arms out, still making that hissing sound, and I wondered if I could get out of the warming house and go for help, get the police, but he was by the door and I was afraid to go past him. Not afraid that he'd do something to me, afraid that I'd hurt him somehow.

So I stood, we stood, and Carl moved his arms even tighter out and the hiss changed to a kind of growl and I realized that he was a plane, a large plane, and I could see it wheeling through the sky, engines rumbling and I knew then that it was a B-17.

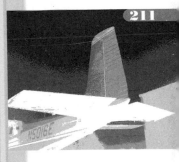

211

Through two, then three loops around the open area in the warming house Carl moved, turning and banking slowly and I swear you could see the plane.

Then something happened. Something hit or hurt the plane, one arm, one wing folded up and over and the plane went down, circling in a great spiral as it went down.

I mean Carl. Carl went down. But it was a plane, too. There in the warming house there was something that Carl did that made him seem a great bomber with a broken wing going down, around and down and I could see it. See the smoke and the explosion as the shell took the wing, the way I'd seen it in newsreels, and then the plane coming down, all the lines coming down, down to the ground in a crash that was like a plane and like a bird, too.

◆◆ Marsh describes Carl as "broken." What does he mean by this?

....

....

....

➥Use the chart below to explore how Carl's experiences in the war changed him. The first excerpt from *Dancing Carl* (in Lesson Two) gives us a glimpse of what Carl might have been like before the war. Use the character traits you brainstormed on page 208 to help you describe what kind of person Carl might have been. Then use the second excerpt to describe what Carl is like as a result of the war.

Before the war	After the war

212

When you read about a character confronting a challenge, try to figure out how and why the experience changes the character.

Four

Challenges in Nature

Characters can face physical challenges as well as personal ones. In many of Gary Paulsen's books, the main characters deal with the challenges of nature—hunger, cold, the fear of being lost. In Paulsen's stories, he not only depicts the struggles characters face, but he also explores what the characters need to do and think in order to survive the challenges.

Dogsong is not a true story, but it is based on Paulsen's own experiences with dog-sledding. The main character, Russel Susskit, is a fourteen-year-old Eskimo boy. Russel becomes friends with Oogruk, an old man who teaches him about dogs, sledding, nature, and the "Old Ways." Russel then goes on a journey of his own, where he meets with many challenges at the hands of nature.

As you read from *Dogsong* (which Paulsen has called his favorite book), put an "X" in the response notes near any parts that focus on challenges in nature.

from **Dogsong** by Gary Paulsen

Response notes ↘

213

When the first dog started to weave with exhaustion, still pulling, but slipping back and forth as it pulled, he sensed their tiredness in the black night and stopped the team. He had a piece of meat in the sled, deer meat from a leg and he cut it in six pieces. When he'd pulled them under an overhanging ledge out of the wind and tipped the sled on its side, he fed them. But they were too tired to eat and slept with the meat between their legs.

He didn't know that they could become that tired and the knowledge frightened him. He was north, in the open, and the dogs wouldn't eat and they were over a hundred and fifty miles to anything. Without the dogs, he would die.

Without the dogs he was nothing.

He'd never felt so alone and for a time fear roared in him. The darkness became an enemy, the cold a killer, the night a ghost from the underworld that would take him down where demons would tear strips off him.

He tried a bite of the meat but he wasn't hungry. Not from tiredness. At least he didn't think so.

But he knew he wasn't thinking too well, and so he lay down between the two wheel-dogs and pulled them close on either side and took a kind of sleep.

Brain-rest more than sleep. He closed his eyes and something inside him rested. The darkness came harder and the northern lights danced and he rested. He was not sure how long it might have been, but it was still dark when one of the dogs got up

← Response notes

and moved in a circle to find a better resting position.

The dog awakened the remainder of the team and they all ate their meat with quiet growls of satisfaction that came from their stomachs up through their throats. Small rumbles that could be felt more than heard.

When they'd eaten they lay down again, not even pausing to relieve themselves. And Russel let them stay down for all of that long night. He dozed now with his eyes open, still between the two wheel-dogs, until the light came briefly.

Then he stood and stretched, feeling the stiffness. The dogs didn't get up and he had to go up the line and lift them. They shook hard to loosen their muscles and drop the tightness of sleeping long.

"Up now! Up and out."

Out.

They started north again, into a land that Russel did not know. At first the dogs ran poorly, raggedly, hating it. But inside half a mile they had settled into their stride and were a working team once more.

But they had lost weight.

In the long run they had lost much weight and it was necessary for Russel to make meat. He didn't know how long they could go without meat but he didn't think it could be long.

He had to hunt.

If he did not get meat the dogs would go down—and he was nothing without the dogs. He had to get food for them.

The light ended the dark-fears but did not bring much warmth. Only the top edge of the sun slipped into view above the horizon, so there was no heat from it.

To get his body warm again after the long night of being still he held onto the sled and ran between the runners. He would run until his breath grew short, then jump on and catch his wind, then run again. It took a few miles of that to get him warm and as soon as he was, the great hole of hunger opened in his stomach and he nearly fell off the sled.

214

●◆ "Without the dogs he was nothing." What do you think Paulsen means by these words?

....

....

....

➽ Choose four challenges in nature that Russel encounters and put them in order from 1 (the most crucial) to 4 (the least crucial). After each challenge, jot down a few ideas to explain why you ranked the challenge as you did. (For example, "It's important to have enough food, but, if Russel doesn't stay warm, he won't be able to hunt.") Compare your chart with others in a small group.

Challenge 1

Challenge 2

215

Challenge 3

Challenge 4

Reading about characters confronting challenges in nature gives us a glimpse of how people act and think when tested by extreme conditions.

Five

Gary Paulsen has based stories on real people and real experiences, but he also wrote about his own experiences in an **autobiography**. In *Woodsong*, he talks about his experiences with his sled dogs and competing in the Iditarod, a grueling sled race across Alaska.

In this selection, Paulsen is describing a time when he burns leftover food to dispose of it—and the smell attracts a big, hungry bear Paulsen calls "Scarhead." As you read the excerpt, think about what Paulsen is learning from the experience. Jot down your ideas in the response notes.

← Response notes

from *Woodsong* by Gary Paulsen

He was having a grand time. The fire didn't bother him. He was trying to reach a paw in around the edges of flame to get at whatever smelled so good. He had torn things apart quite a bit—ripped one side off the burn enclosure—and I was having a bad day and it made me mad.

I was standing across the burning fire from him and without thinking—because I was so used to him—I picked up a stick, threw it at him, and yelled, "Get out of here."

I have made many mistakes in my life, and will probably make many more, but I hope never to throw a stick at a bear again.

In one rolling motion—the muscles seemed to move within the skin so fast that I couldn't take half a breath—he turned and came for me. Close. I could smell his breath and see the red around the sides of his eyes. Close on me he stopped and raised on his back legs and hung over me, his forelegs and paws hanging down, weaving back and forth gently as he took his time and decided whether or not to tear my head off.

I could not move, would not have time to react. I knew I had nothing to say about it. One blow would break my neck. Whether I lived or died depended on him, on his thinking, on his ideas about me—whether I was worth the bother or not.

I did not think then.

Looking back on it I don't remember having one coherent thought when it was happening. All I knew was terrible menace. His eyes looked very small as he studied me. He looked down on me for what seemed hours. I did not move, did not breathe, did not think or do anything.

And he lowered.

Perhaps I was not worth the trouble. He lowered slowly and turned back to the trash and I walked backward halfway to the house and then ran—anger growing now—and took the rifle from the gun rack by the door and came back out.

216

from *Woodsong* by Gary Paulsen

He was still there, rummaging through the trash. I worked the bolt and fed a cartridge in and aimed at the place where you kill bears and began to squeeze. In raw anger, I began to take up the four pounds of pull necessary to send death into him.

And stopped.

Kill him for what?

That thought crept in.

Kill him for what?

For not killing me? For letting me know it is wrong to throw sticks at four-hundred-pound bears? For not hurting me, for not killing me, I should kill him? I lowered the rifle and ejected the shell and put the gun away. I hope Scarhead is still alive. For what he taught me, I hope he lives long and is very happy because I learned then—looking up at him while he made up his mind whether or not to end me—that when it is all boiled down I am nothing more and nothing less than any other animal in the woods.

Response notes

●◆ Compare Paulsen's experience with the bear to a challenge faced by one of the characters in his novels. Use the chart below to record your ideas.

Paulsen's Challenge	How Paulsen Changed

Character's Challenge	How Character Changed

●◆Think about a challenging experience that you have faced. Write notes for your own autobiography. Describe the experience, what you learned from it, and how it changed you.

Experience:

What happened:

What I learned from it:

Writers share events from their own lives not only to tell what happened, but also to tell what makes those events important.

10, 11 Excerpts from *Roll of Thunder, Hear My Cry* by Mildred D. Taylor. Copyright © 1976 by Mildred D. Taylor. Used by permission of Dial Books for Young Readers, a division of Penguin Putnam Inc.

14 Excerpt from *The Gold Cadillac* by Mildred D. Taylor. Copyright ©1987 by Mildred D. Taylor. Used by permission of Dial Books for Young Readers, a division of Penguin Putnam Inc.

20 Excerpt from *The Friendship* by Mildred D. Taylor. Copyright ©1987 by Mildred D. Taylor. Used by permission of Dial Books for Young Readers, a division of Penguin Putnam Inc.

22 From *Roll of Thunder Hear My Cry* by Mildred D. Taylor. Copyright © 1976 by Mildred D. Taylor. Used by permission of Dial Books for Young Readers, a division of Penguin Putnam Inc.

26, 29 "All Summer in a Day" by Ray Bradbury. Reprinted by permission of Don Congdon Associates, Inc. Copyright ©1954, renewed 1982 by Ray Bradbury.

33 "It's All In How You Say It" by Mickey Roberts, from *Talking Leaves*. Used by permission of author.

36 "Holiday Dinner" from *The Song in My Head* by Felice Holman. Reprinted with the permission of Atheneum Books for Young Readers, an imprint of Simon & Schuster Children's Publishing Division. Text copyright ©1985 Felice Holman.

40 Excerpt from *The Search for Delicious* by Natalie Babbitt. Copyright ©1969 and copyright renewed © 1997 by Natalie Babbitt. Reprinted by permission of Farrar, Straus & Giroux, Inc.

40 Excerpt from *A Wrinkle in Time* by Madeleine L'Engle. Copyright ©1962 and copyright renewed ©1990 by Crosswicks Ltd. Reprinted by permission of Farrar, Straus & Giroux, Inc.

42, 45 Excerpt from *Danny: the Champion of the World* by Roald Dahl. Copyright ©1975 by Roald Dahl and Alfred A. Knopf, Inc. Reprinted by permission of Alfred A. Knopf, Inc.

48 "A Game of Catch" by Richard Wilbur. Copyright ©1994 by Richard Wilbur, reprinted by permission of Harcourt Brace & Company. Originally appeared in *The New Yorker.*

56, 60 "Utzel and His Daughter Poverty" from *When Shlemiel Went to Warsaw* by Isaac Bashevis Singer, pictures by Margot Zemach. Translation copyright ©1968 by Isaac Bashevis Singer and Elizabeth Shub. Pictures copyright © by Margot Zemach. Reprinted by permission of Farrar, Straus & Giroux, Inc.

63 Excerpt from *One-Eyed Cat* by Paula Fox. Reprinted with the permission of Simon & Schuster Books for Young Readers, an imprint of Simon & Schuster Children's Publishing Division. Copyright ©1984 Paula Fox.

66 Excerpt from *Seedfolks* by Paul Fleischman. Text Copyright ©1988 by Paul Fleischman. Used by permission of HarperCollins Publishers.

69 Excerpt from *Beethoven Lives Upstairs* by Barbara Nichol, illustrated by Scott Cameron. Text copyright ©1993 by Classical Productions for Children Limited. Reprinted by permission of Orchard Books, New York.

74 "maggie and milly and molly and may" from *Complete Poems: 1904–1962* by E. E. Cummings, edited by George J. Firmage. Copyright ©1956, 1984, 1991 by the Trustees for the E. E. Cummings Trust, Reprinted by permission of Liveright Publishing Corporation.

76 "Grape Sherbet" by Rita Dove. Copyright ©1983 by Rita Dove. Used by permission of the author.

81 "Telephone Talk" from *The Kite That Braved Old Orchard Beach* by X. J. Kennedy. Reprinted with the permission of Margaret K. McElderry Books, an imprint of Simon & Schuster Children's Publishing Division Text copyright ©1991 X. J. Kennedy.

84 "Almost Perfect" by Shel Silverstein. Copyright ©1981 By Evil Eye Music, Inc. Used by permission of HarperCollins Publishers.

88 "A Uniformly Good Idea" by Steve Forbes. Reprinted by permission of *Forbes Magazine* © Forbes Inc., 1994.

93 "Robots Will Never Replace Humans" by Rosa Velasquez from *English* by E. Sulzby, et al. Copyright ©1989 by McGraw-Hill, Inc. Reprinted with permission of The McGraw-Hill Companies.

96 "Endangered is a Scary Word" from *Green Planet Rescue* by Robert R. Halpern, published by Franklin Watts. Copyright © 1993 by The Zoological Society of Cincinnati, Inc. Reprinted by permission of Grolier Publishing Co.

100, 103 Excerpts from *A Summer to Die* by Lois Lowry. Copyright ©1977 by Lois Lowry. Reprinted by permission of Houghton Mifflin Co. All rights reserved.

106 Excerpt from *Autumn Street* by Lois Lowry. Copyright ©1980 by Lois Lowry. Reprinted by permission of Houghton Mifflin Co. All rights reserved.

109 Excerpt from *Number the Stars* by Lois Lowry. Copyright ©1989 by Lois Lowry. Reprinted by permission of Houghton Mifflin Co. All rights reserved.

113 Lois Lowry's Newbery acceptance speech from *The Horn Book Magazine*, Jul/Aug 1990, reprinted by permission of The Horn Book, Inc., 11 Beacon St., Suite 1000, Boston, MA 02108.

116, 118 Excerpts from *And Then There Was One* by Margery Facklam. Text Copyright ©1990 by Margery Facklam; Illustrations Copyright ©1990 by Pamela Johnson. By permission of Little, Brown and Company.

121 Excerpt from "A Personal Narrative" by Kim-Hue Phan is used by permission of the author.

123 Excerpt from *An Owl In the House* by Alice Calaprice. Text adaptation copyright ©1990 Alice Calaprice. By permission of Little, Brown and Company.

126 Excerpt from *Experimenting with Inventions* by Robert Gardner. Copyright ©1990. Reprinted by permission of Grolier Publishing Co.

130, 134 Excerpts from *World: Adventures in Time and Place* by James A. Banks, et al. (McGraw-Hill, Inc.). Reprinted by permission of McGraw-Hill, Inc.

136 Excerpt from *The Ancient Egyptians* by Elsa Marston. Reprinted by Permission of Marshall Cavendish.

139, 141 Excerpts from *Egyptian Pyramids* by Anne Steel. By permission of Wayland Ltd.

144 Excerpt from *Can It Really Rain Frogs?: The World's Strangest Weather Events* by Spencer Christian and Antonia Felix. Copyright ©1997. Reprinted by permission of John Wiley & Sons, Inc.

148, 151 Excerpts from *The Titanic* by Richard Wormser. Copyright ©1994 by Parachute Press, New York, NY.

155 Excerpt from *It's Our World, Too!* by Phillip Hoose. Copyright ©1993 by Phillip Hoose. By permission of Little, Brown and Company.

160 "let there be new flowering" by Lucille Clifton from *Good Woman: Poems and a Memoir, 1969–1980.* Copyright ©1987 by Lucille Clifton. Reprinted with the permission of BOA Editions, Ltd. 260 East Ave., Rochester, NY 14604.

162 "Waking from a Nap on the Beach" from *The Complete Poems to Solve* by May Swenson. Reprinted with the permission of Simon & Schuster Books for Young Readers, an imprint of Simon & Schuster Children's Publishing Division Copyright ©1993 by the Literary Estate of May Swenson.

165 Excerpt from *Maniac Magee* by Jerry Spinelli. Copyright ©1990 by Jerry Spinelli. By permission of Little, Brown and Company.

171 "The Courage That My Mother Had" by Edna St. Vincent Millay from *Collected Poems,* HarperCollins. Copyright ©1954, 1982 by Norma Millay Ellis. All rights reserved. Reprinted by permission of Elizabeth Barnett, literary executor.

174 "Lineage" by Margaret Walker from *This Is My Century: New and Collected Poems*. Copyright ©1989. By permission of The University of Georgia Press.

176 "Finding a Lucky Number" by Gary Soto from *New and Selected Poems.* Copyright ©1995, published by Chronicle Books, San Francisco.

178 "There is No Word for Goodbye" from *The Light on the Tent Wall* by Mary TallMountain. Reprinted by permission of the American Indian Studies Center, UCLA. Copyright © Regents of the University of California.

181 "Adventures of Isabel" from *Custard and Company* by Ogden Nash. Copyright ©1957 by Ogden Nash. By permission Little, Brown and Company.

184 "Life Doesn't Frighten Me" from *And I Still Rise* by Maya Angelou. Copyright ©1978 by Maya Angelou. Reprinted by permission of Random House, Inc.

189, 192 "Hearing the Sweetest Songs" by Nicolette Toussaint from *Newsweek,* May 23, 1994. All rights reserved. Reprinted by permission.

195 "The Myth of the Computer" by Steven Levy from *Newsweek,* Special Issue Winter ©1997, *Newsweek,* Inc. All Rights reserved. Reprinted by permission.

200 Excerpt from *All I Really Need to Know I Learned in Kindergarten* by Robert L. Fulghum. Copyright ©1986, 1988 by Robert L. Fulghum. Reprinted by permission of Villard Books, a division of Random House, Inc.

204 Excerpt from *The River* by Gary Paulsen. Copyright ©1991 by Gary Paulsen. Used by permission of Delacorte Press, a division of Bantam Doubleday Dell Publishing Group, Inc.

207, 210 Excerpts from *Dancing Carl* by Gary Paulsen. Reprinted with the permission of Simon & Schuster Books for Young Readers, an imprint of Simon & Schuster Children's Publishing Division Copyright ©1983 Gary Paulsen.

213 Excerpt from *Dogsong* by Gary Paulsen. Reprinted with the permission of Simon & Schuster Books for Young Readers, an imprint of Simon & Schuster Children's Publishing Division Copyright ©1983 Gary Paulsen.

216 Excerpt from *Woodsong* by Gary Paulsen. Reprinted with the permission of Simon & Schuster Books for Young Readers, an imprint of Simon & Schuster Children's Publishing Division Copyright © 1983 Gary Paulsen.

Every effort has been made to secure complete rights and permissions for each literary excerpt presented herein. Updated acknowledgments will appear in subsequent printings.

Design: Christine Ronan Design

Photographs: Unless otherwise noted below, all photographs are the copyrighted work of Mel Hill.

Front and Back Covers: © Peter Adams/Masterfile

9 © Jill Sabella/FPG International

25 © Andy Roberts/Tony Stone Images

39 © Tim Windsor/Tony Stone Images

55 © Jean-Francoise Gate/Tony Stone Images

73 © Uwe Starke/Masterfile

87 © I. Burgum / P. Boorman/Tony Stone Images

99 © UPI/Corbis-Bettman

115 © Peter Cole/Bruce Coleman Inc.

129 © UPI/Corbis-Bettman

143 © Jeff Foott/Bruce Coleman Inc.

159 © Will & Deni McIntyre/Tony Stone Images

173 © Myron Taplin/Tony Stone Images

187 © Robert Holmgren/Tony Stone Images

203 © Brian Bailey/Tony Stone Images

Picture Research: Feldman and Associates

Glossary

alliteration, the repetition of the same consonant sound at the beginning of words.

assonance, the repetition of vowel sounds across syllables or words. Assonance is a characteristic of POETRY.

audience, those people who read or hear what a writer has written.

author's perspective, a way of looking at a subject or a work of literature. An author's perspective can be influenced by background knowledge and experiences.

author's purpose, the reason why an author writes. Authors write to entertain, to inform or explain, to persuade or argue, or to express personal thoughts or feelings.

autobiography, an author's account of his or her own life.

bias, favoring (and often presenting) one side of an argument.

biography, the story of a person's life written by another person.

cause and effect, a relationship that exists when one event (the cause) brings about the other event (the effect).

change pace, a reading strategy in which the reader adjusts the rate of reading (slows down or speeds up) depending on the reading material and purpose for reading.

characterization, the method an author uses to reveal or describe characters and their various personalities and motives.

characters, people, animals, or imaginary creatures in a story.

connotation, the emotional meaning of a word in addition to its dictionary meaning.

consonance, repetition of consonant sounds across syllables or words. Consonance is a characteristic of POETRY.

context clues, a vocabulary strategy in which the reader looks at the words around an unfamiliar word to find clues to its meaning.

denotation, the exact, "dictionary" definition of a word.

description, writing that paints a colorful picture of a person, place, thing, or idea using concrete, vivid DETAILS.

details, words from a description that elaborate on subjects, characters, or action in a work. Sensory details are generally vivid, colorful, and appeal to the senses.

dialogue, the talking that goes on between CHARACTERS in a story.

editorial, a brief persuasive article in a newspaper expressing an opinion.

fact, something that can be proven to be true.

fiction, writing that tells an imaginary story.

figurative language, language used to create a special effect or feeling. Figurative language goes beyond the literal meanings of the words used. SIMILE, METAPHOR, and PERSONIFICATION are examples of figurative language.

highlight, to underline, circle, or mark the information that is most important as you read.

historical fiction, writing that combines historical FACTS and fictional DETAILS.

221

imagery, the words or phrases a writer uses to describe or present objects, feelings, actions, ideas, etc. Imagery is usually based on SENSORY LANGUAGE.

inference, a reasonable guess based upon information provided in a piece of writing.

irony (situational), the contrast between what characters or readers might reasonably expect to happen and what actually happens.

journal, a daily record of thoughts, impressions, and autobiographical information. A journal can be a source for ideas about writing.

main idea, the central point or purpose in a piece of NONFICTION.

metaphor, comparison of two unlike things without using a word of comparison such as *like* or *as*. Example: "The stars were diamonds."

222

meter, a poem's RHYTHM.

mood, the feeling(s) a story gives readers. Examples: happy, peaceful, sad.

narrator, the writer or speaker who tells the story or describes events in the story.

nonfiction, writing that tells a true story or explores an idea. There are many categories of nonfiction, including autobiography, biography, and essay.

onomatopoeia, words that sound like what they mean. Examples: buzz, crackle, hiss.

opinion, a person's personal ideas about a subject. An opinion cannot be proven true or false.

personification, a form of FIGURATIVE LANGUAGE in which an idea, object, or animal is given human characteristics. Example: "The rock stubbornly refused to move."

persuasion, writing that is meant to change the way the reader thinks or acts.

plot, the action or sequence of events in a story.

poetry, an imaginative kind of writing that tells a story, describes an experience, or reflects on an idea. It is usually characterized by STANZAS rather than paragraphs; it uses RHYTHM, FIGURATIVE LANGUAGE, SENSORY DETAILS, and sometimes RHYME.

point of view, the angle from which a story is told. A first-person point of view means that one of the characters is telling the story. Example: "I was angry when I left the shop, and I'm sure Leo was too." A third-person point of view means that someone outside the story is telling it. Example: "The two boys were angry when they left the shop."

predict, to use what you already know in order to guess what will happen in the future.

preview, to skim or scan before reading in order to become familiar with the topic or the text.

repetition, a figure of speech in which a word, phrase, or idea is repeated for emphasis and effect in a piece of literature.

rhyme, the similarity of sound at the end of two or more words. Rhyme is a characteristic of POETRY.

rhythm, the ordered occurrence of sound in POETRY.

sensory language, language that appeals to the five senses: sight, sound, taste, smell, and touch.

sequence, the order of events.

setting, the time and place of a story.

short story, a brief fictional narrative.

simile, a comparison of two unlike objects using *like* or *as*. Example: "The sun rose like a giant flower out of the sky."

stanza, a group of lines that are set off to form a division in POETRY.

structural clues, a vocabulary strategy in which the reader breaks down an unfamiliar word and uses familiar parts, such as the prefix, root word, or suffix, to help determine the word's meaning.

style, how an author uses words, phrases, and sentences to form his or her ideas.

summarize, to restate briefly the most important parts of a piece of writing in your own words.

text structure, the way writing is organized.

theme, the statement about life or human nature that an author wants to make to the reader.

tone, the writer's attitude toward a subject. A writer's tone can be serious, sarcastic, objective, etc.

viewpoint, an author's opinion on a particular subject.

visualize, to see or picture in your mind what you read.

224